CHILDREN'S
Special Places

Landscapes of Childhood

General Editor

Elizabeth N. Goodenough
Residential College, University of Michigan

Editorial Board

CHILDREN'S
Special Places

Exploring the Role of Forts, Dens,
and Bush Houses in Middle Childhood

David Sobel, M.Ed.

Wayne State University Press   Detroit

Originally published in 1993 by Zephyr Press

Wood engravings by Randy Miller; used with permission.

Copyright © 2002 by Wayne State University Press,
Detroit, Michigan 48201. All rights are reserved.
No part of this book may be reproduced without formal permission.
Manufactured in the United States of America.

ISBN-13: 978-0-8143-3026-5   ISBN-10: 0-8143-3026-6

A catalog record for this book is available from the Library of Congress.

CONTENTS

FOREWORD

How societies use and create spaces for children—day care centers, schools, theme parks, video games—determines how the next generation will see reality. Those who design software for kids or the play areas at fast food restaurants replicate some mental picture of users' joy. Conceptions of childhood past, present, and future and the corresponding worlds constructed by adults "for the kids" revolve around such issues as innocence and deviance, safety and abuse, contemporary kinderculture, and the "disappearance" of childhood. However, in our highly programmed and commercial world, little is known about why children gravitate to certain locales for comfort, excitement, self-awareness, or beauty and avoid other areas. Entomologist

E. O. Wilson considers the early quest to construct secret space a "fundamental trait of human nature" of "ulti-mate value to survival." Yet this primal urge has largely escaped notice.

David Sobel's *Children's Special Places* makes a novel contribution to the small but growing movement which pays heed to our need for play. His investigation of the role of forts, dens, and bush houses for children growing up in Devon, England, the island of Carriacou, West Indies, and rural and urban parts of the United States provides intimate access to a highly personal but little-studied zone of human experience. "Sometimes I make a little playhouse for myself, I bring things to eat and read books" (Dwight, age 10). "'My secret den,' he whis-pered. 'No one knows about this place, even my broth-er'" (Alex). "I wanted me to go in it, but not other peo-ple" (Nechole, age 11). Such voices document a rare view of how the young seek refuge from grown-up soci-ety in realms that paradoxically ease their way into adulthood. Children know the importance of hiding out, of finding the "just for me" place where they cannot be seen. Peeking through a hollowed-out hedgerow or climbing a tree is the initial discovery of a "self-ish" space, a site detached from the ongoing intimate relation with parents, siblings, teachers, or peers. Playing house or capturing insects in small, cupped hands, children reframe the universe, teasing their imagination to find its own dimensions.

We like to imagine that when this place of discovery is outdoors, kids will find that the best things in life are still free: sand, air, trees, animals, water. Too many of our assumptions about childhood reflect romantic ideals of the past, not the white noise of today's advertising and mass media, which assault children with labels and "lifestyles." Fewer than two percent of Americans now grow up in the country. The high-rise housing projects of the 1950s offered playscapes of asphalt, metal jungle gyms, and concrete towers; today the relentless destruction of vegetation by developers and the malling of recreational spaces indicate how little adults sincerely care about children's contact with living things or the social isolation of the very poor. Issues of land use now attract public interest and debate. Yet architects, real estate developers, and city planners remain half blind to ways the young relate to their physical surroundings in unstructured settings; rarely do they consider the needs of low-caste children or those for whom home is not safe. Millions of young people are growing up on sterile streets without backyards or safe parks. As vicarious pursuits, virtual pets, and synthetic playgrounds become pervasive, a world that allows minimal emotional engagement with animals and plants may be threatening to nature itself.

Although a wide range of theories has been proposed to explain global transformations in politics, economics, and the environment over the last decade, children are seldom given space to reflect on the societies in which they live or the kind of play they like. Vagrant minors around the world search for safety in hideaways, and street children from Cairo to Bogota to Seoul are seen but not heard. Building on Edith Cobb's *The Ecology of the Imagination in Childhood* and Roger Hart's *Children's Experience of Place*, this volume awakens our awareness of how children, who own nothing, possess places. Examining the critical role of hideouts in middle childhood, Sobel's cross-cultural research in environmental education suggests that between the ages of six and twelve what girls and boys want most of all is to "make a world in which to find a place to discover a self." However humble the shelter, these first getaways and solo vantage points live on in memory and imagination. Adults come to connect these havens with dreams or their quest for islands of rebirth and reform. But because grown-ups do not often recall what they most cherished and desired as children, Sobel's candor about his own early life and recollections by such nature writers as Kim Stafford create a dramatic entry into the subject. Sobel's clear, unpretentious voice, a rarity in literary and education circles, prevails through the description of his research, examination of theory, and survey of educational experiments and practices. His speculations suggest an ideal of human development which embraces continuity of childhood promise and fosters respect for space, both private and communal.

Research on worldbuilding in childhood is obviously fraught with difficulty. The very acts of writing and reading about shaping secret worlds can erase or distort unique experience. A sensitivity to the need for privacy informs Sobel's methodology, which keeps close to what is freely offered and is nuanced by the understanding "that there are realms in which the adult should not trespass" (116). His orientation is pragmatic and poetic, and it encompasses perspectives of developmental psychology, literary studies, pedagogy, environmental concerns, and social justice. An ethnographer, not a statistician, Sobel relies primarily on direct observation and anecdotal narrative. However, the implications of his map-and-interview technique touch on a wide range of landmark studies and conceptual models, including those of C. G. Jung, Robert Coles, and Joseph Chilton Pearce, to explain how our comfort zones influence human lives and learning.

As he reassesses various cultural constructions of childhood, Sobel's multicultural perspective shows respect for differences and finds likenesses important to developmental psychology. When we force children to live in ugly and dangerous areas, we assault them and their future at the most basic level. In the complex ecology of growing up, however, children today can be impoverished in many different ways. Play is increasingly moving indoors and on screen or into commercial and corporate realms. Other families, "stranger danger," and our own backyards are perceived as potential hazards, yet children, even those in gated communities, are able to gain access in cyberspace to zones once off-limits to adults.

From an educational standpoint, the demand for risk-free playgrounds, the "excellence" associated with standarized testing, and the development of a so-called common culture erode informal learning situations. Many schools have cut recess from the curriculum, and some new schools are being built without playgrounds. "Learning with technology is a priority, because it is what society expects of our children," trumpets a headline of the *U.S. Department of Education Community*

Update (May 2001). As Sobel makes us see, though, constructing a multimedia homepage, even in high resolution, is not the same as exploration and placemaking outdoors. Technology can encourage the excitement of intellectual exploration: 10-year-olds can dig for facts and even create knowledge. Yet young humans do not just crave information. They also seek to put together what they see and have heard and to make forays into worlds of their own. Stories children tell, like secret hideouts, cultivate a hedge between inner and outer spheres that brings the two worlds into synchrony both in language and in space. Putting such structures on life, getting inside these enclosed spaces, is primal play. In the tactile and sensory richness of outdoors, girls and boys can insist on the logic of an area that is "all for me" while scripting what they look for and become.

As the need for afterschool programs becomes acute, community-based participatory research must be serious and ongoing. *Children's Special Places* makes a significant contribution to the interdisciplinary conversation about the importance of place and play in children's lives. What should be the respective roles of children, teachers, and community members in the debate about funding and services for time out of school? How does the evidence children provide compare to other ways of

knowing? How does the fantasy space of literature connect to the actual space occupied by children in their
play? Does it make a difference in a young life when
lawns are replaced by asphalt? Given the rapid development of children's studies, Sobel's work should inspire
school boards and practitioners, community and civic
leaders to preserve semiwild sanctuaries for free play,
enabling children to rediscover ways of learning outside.

The Child and the City series is concerned with sup-
porting the environment, health, education, culture,
recreation and legal rights of urban childhoods. As our
sense of endangered survival on this shrinking planet
becomes acute, children are our last frontier. They represent twenty percent of our population but one hundred
percent of our future. To the degree that we can envision
children as triumphant go-betweens or heroic survivors,
they shelter the imagination and sustain the hope of
adults. Yet the bodies and minds of children—the very
spaces they inhabit—are under assault. Cuts in public
funding have altered lives. Firearms kill fifteen children
in the United States daily, and incidents of violence are
changing the rules of the game at elementary as well as
middle schools and high schools. Making visible what
has typically remained unseen in children's lives,

Children's Special Places occupies an important place in the documentary tradition. It has been included in The Child and the City series because it moves beyond the boundaries of specialized discourse to engage a wide audience—ecological critics, environmental life writers, play therapists, academics in children's studies, parents, teachers, homeschoolers, museum staffs, parks and recreation staffs, urban planners, and playground designers. Broadening the space for reconstructions of childhood imaginatively, institutionally, internationally, in legal as well as academic and poetic discourse, is the goal of this series. Sobel's volume holds a mirror up to us, the people who form the human and material environment of children.

—Elizabeth N. Goodenough

1
THE SEARCH

AUTOBIOGRAPHICAL PRELUDE

The fort at Sterling's house called to me each time I passed by on the way to the bus stop. Snuggled into the pine duff underneath the looming trees, the structure grew up out of the soil like a mushroom. An organic presence hovered around it; the fort belonged here as did the squirrels and rabbits. The branches, pieces of plywood, sod, and fiberglass roofing from which it was built had all grown together. An amalgamation of mold and cobwebs filled the uneven gaps between the boards, eliminating the penetration of all unwanted, intrusive light.

As a small, naive second grader in a neighborhood dominated by a gang of fourth and fifth graders, I was a non-initiate in fort ways. Access to the fort was closely guarded. I'm sure there must have been a password. Sterling ruled over the lair and over many of the community children and activities. He was three years older than I, and I lived in fear of his domination.

But I wanted membership in the club and my desire made me a potential victim. I always got fifty cents to pay for school lunch. If I planned my purchases well, I could manage to clear lunchtime and arrive at the general store where the bus stopped with anywhere from six to fifteen cents. A Popsicle cost six cents; a Snickers bar was a dime. Sometime during my second-grade year, Sterling figured out that I was a potential source of cash. Capitalizing on my fear and his size, he started charging me protection money. If I paid him ten cents every day, he might let me join the rest of the boys inside the fort *and* I would be guaranteed safe passage home. Of course, he was the only person I had to worry about. I lived in fear of this daily extortion, my travail shared with no one. And I remember with exhilaration the day I stepped off the bus and ran for home without paying—the spell of fear was broken.

But a spell still hovered around the fort. And despite, or perhaps as a result of, my flaunting of Sterling's authority,

I finally did get invited inside. One grey autumn afternoon, Mickey, a first grader, and I were brought along by the crowd of older boys. We leaped at the chance to be part of the action. The entrance tunnel led to a countless number of dark rooms and to a central chamber where schemes were hatched, matches lit. It smelled earthy, smoky, and secret. But just as we were starting to feel the thrill of being a member of the club, we realized we were the day's entertainment. *"Take off your pants!"* Sterling ordered. We had no choice. Everyone laughed as we sat around in our Fruit of the Looms. *"Now get out of here,"* he ordered. He wanted us to walk home in our underwear! I was horrified. *"But . . ."* we resisted, and I think we were pushed out of the tunnel into the cold, grey afternoon.

I have two clear parallel memories of what happened then. One memory has me darting from bush to hedge wearing only my underwear and slipping in the back door of my house, defeated and embarrassed. The other is of me pleading and groveling enough to get my pants back and then being laughed out of the fort. I'm still not sure which memory is actually true. But I am sure that, in spite of this embarrassment, the private, world-with-its-own-rules feeling of the fort still exerted a hold on me.

OVERVIEW

This scene comes back to me as I review my memories of "forts," the private and group hideouts of childhood. There are others: the labyrinthine passages in the rhododendrons, the leaf houses underneath the maple, the shaded space between the curved brick wall and the tree where I went by myself to read and look out over Long Island Sound. It has become clear to me that these places are almost a universal experience of childhood.

From my work as a teacher of elementary school children, graduate students in education and environmental studies, and elementary and secondary teachers, I have long been aware of the phenomenon of forts in American children's culture. I have found them in the backyards of New England and on the banks of Florida's Suwanee River, from the urban woodlands of Washington's Rock Creek Park to the dry canyons of Los Angeles's expensive suburbs. Roger Hart's portrayal of children's experience of the Vermont landscape in *Children's Experience of Place* provides a superb documentation of the centrality of fort building for elementary-age children in rural America.[1] But now I have the sense that forts are a part of children's experience in rural and urban settings around the globe.

6

From September 1987 to May 1988, I took a leave of absence from my position as chairperson of the Education Department at Antioch/New England Graduate School. I had two objectives. First, I wanted to explore new landscapes with my wife and my one-year-old daughter. Second, I wanted to explore the affective geography of elementary-age children in places other than my native New England. I wanted to understand the way in which other children see and experience their landscapes.

I was motivated by a variety of questions. What places are special? Which places have most personal meaning? Which areas are most intriguing, most evocative of imaginative responses? What do children do, and where do they go when they have free time? My plan was to use this portrait of children's geographic interests as a basis for curriculum development and evaluation. I was looking for the building blocks of the foundation upon which geography, environmental education, and social studies curricula could be built.

My study sites were consciously chosen to be as different from one another as possible. My intent was to look for constant elements in children's geographies in very different cultures and landscapes. Similarities would suggest universal aspects of children's experience—the biological and psychological foundations for curriculum.

7

THE PLACES AND THE CHILDREN

From September to December 1987, I worked with all ninety children, aged five through eleven, in the Denbury Primary School in Devon, England. This school draws children predominantly from the villages of Denbury and Ogwell, both within about four miles of Newton Abbot, a market town of approximately 20,000 people. The communities are nestled into the rolling farm country of south Devon, and children come from a balance of agricultural, building trades, and professional families. All children in the school were white except for one black West Indian girl. Approximately 60 percent of the children lived in new housing developments, 20 percent on farms or in rural areas, and 20 percent in old village housing.

Denbury is located on the edge of Dartmoor National Park; the hills and granite spires of Dartmoor are visible from throughout the village. Autumns are wet, windy, and cool, and the landscape is a mix of agricultural land and protected woodlands. Small streams and brooks lace the rolling countryside. Though many children lived in new, large housing estates, open fields and forests were easily accessible to all the children in my study group. Rambling through the countryside was a common pastime for most of the children I worked with.

From January through May 1988, I worked with 101 of the 125 children aged five through fifteen in the Harvey Vale Government School located on the island of Carriacou in the West Indies. The school draws children predominantly from the communities of Harvey Vale and Belmont. Most children live within a mile of school. Both communities are located on a band of impoverished agricultural land between the ocean and steep hills that rise to almost 1,000 feet. All children in the school were black except for one white Italian girl.

Carriacou is the largest of the Grenadines, a string of small islands that stretch from Grenada to St. Vincent in the lower Windward Islands. Carriacou is politically part of the nation of Grenada and has a population of approximately 6,000 residents.

January through June is the dry season on Carriacou. As the hills of the island are not high enough to comb rainwater from passing clouds, the island becomes parched as the dry season progresses. Trees lose their leaves, the hills become brown, and many families experience water shortages. Only a few freshwater ponds exist on the island, but almost all children live within walking distance of the coast. Coastal landforms range from protected sandy beaches to rocky cliffs.

Carriacou is different from many Caribbean islands because it is not dominated by a tourist culture. This means there is not a glaring discrepancy between rich and poor and that the people have managed to retain a substantial portion of their cultural heritage. The dance and festival traditions can be traced to their African tribal origins, and there is a still-active boat-building tradition. Most people are poor but not impoverished. In great part, this is a subsistence economy moving very slowly to a cash economy. All families grow a substantial portion of their food, fish, and raise animals. Children become involved in these processes very early, beginning to shell peas when they are four and raise animals when they are six.

In summary, the children and landscapes could not have been more different. In England, the children came to school in pressed grey flannel slacks and skirts with white shirts, ties for the boys, polished shoes, and red school sweaters. In Carriacou, children wore tattered shirts and beige shorts or blue skirts, and they were often barefoot. In England, the building was stuffed with curriculum materials—there was even a voluntary keyboard class. In Carriacou, there were holes in the floor, barely enough paper and pencils, and no running water. In England, it was always cloudy and blustery, the landscape green and ivy-covered. In Carriacou it was glaringly bright and hot, the landscape dusty and prickly with cactus and acacia. Yet despite these and many other differences, there were some striking similarities in the children's landscape activities.

Not far into my mapmaking and interviews with children in England, "dens" started to crop up on children's maps. Because I am familiar with the notion of "forts" in the United States, I think the first few references slipped by me. When I probed, I discovered a variety of terms, including *bases, houses, treehouses,* and *treeforts* that referred to children's special places.

Though there were some differences between boys' and girls' forts, these places were significant for both genders. One group of girls brought me to the site of their old Explorer's Club; I was disappointed it had fallen prey to the expansion of the local housing development. Certainly "Wendy houses" are institutionalized in many British classrooms. One existed in the infant classroom for five- and six-year-olds in Denbury Primary School. These little housekeeping corners or playhouses were inspired by the house Peter Pan's gang built for their new "mother," Wendy. Recall the song, *"Let's be quiet as a mouse/and build a tiny little house/for Wendy."* But the dens and houses these children referred to were all personally found or constructed in the landscape.

Arriving in Carriacou, I wondered whether this

phenomenon would be central to children's experience in this completely different culture and place. In my initial interviews with children, I was careful not to ask explicitly about these places, but waited instead to see if they emerged in the children's maps and interviews. Sure enough, in the second week, a boy named Dwight said, *"Sometimes I build a little playhouse for myself."* It turned out that this term tended to be used by younger boys and girls. They also referred to "houses" and "playshops" regularly. Most interesting to me were "bush houses," referred to by all ages but most popular among older boys. These places seemed most comparable to the British "dens" and American "forts."

From my discussions with adults in England and Carriacou, and my work with children and teachers in the United States, I have learned that forts, dens, and bush houses have been prevalent in children's experience for many generations. After my presentation to teachers in training in Exmouth, Devon, an African student of Ikung bushman heritage commented on how similar his experience was as a child growing up in the Kalahari. They, too, built bush houses at a distance from the village complex.

Assuming, then, that found and built spaces are a nearly universal component of children's landscape experience, I want to elaborate on the role these spaces play in the evolving self of the child. To explore the child's landscape and the implications for education, I will:

* describe specific examples of children's houses, dens, and bush houses from England and Carriacou;

* portray the role these places play during middle childhood in helping to foster and shape the unique self that is born in adolescence;

* examine adult perspectives on the role these places have played in their lives via interviews and literature;

* provide working examples of elementary school curricula that translate children's place-making interests into projects that expand their sense of self and their knowledge of the social and natural world.

2
ENTERING THE CHILD'S WORLD

THE DENS OF DEVON

My work with children in Devon was organized into two phases. From September through November, I visited Denbury Primary School twice a week. During the day I met with three or four children at a time for periods of approximately one hour and fifteen minutes. They drew maps and I interviewed each one during this time. Each child worked alone at a table. Children were selected randomly, but I made an effort not to have siblings and neighbors working simultaneously. This separation was important to ensure that individual children arrived at their map images independently. When the same special places later showed up on maps of children from the same neighborhood, I could be assured it wasn't because they had copied from each other.

17

From November through December, I conducted field trips and explorations with children during the school day. I selected a representative sample of twenty-eight children, an equal number of boys and girls, drawn from all age levels, for these walks. I chose children on the basis of their interest in the project and for the purposes of exploring common areas of interest that cropped up on different children's maps. The school was helpful in arranging these field trips, and parents were notified prior to their occurrence.

THE MAP-AND-INTERVIEW TECHNIQUE

My instructions were open-ended and fairly simple, modified only slightly for younger children:

I am writing a book for teachers about children's neighborhoods and children's maps. I'd like you to help me with my project. Today I'd like you to draw a map of your neighborhood. By neighborhood, I mean the area around your house where you spend most of your time and where you play. The only thing you have to include on your map is your own house. Beyond that, it's up to you to show me the places that are special or important to you. It's fine to show other houses, but be sure to include your special places. Your map can include everywhere you are allowed to travel by yourself or with friends, but if you want to show a smaller area, that's fine. Work on your own map, and please don't talk with others while you are working.

I always first asked for a map because I was interested in the developmental emergence of the map concept independent from my interest in children's special places.

When younger children appeared puzzled by the notion of a map, I said, "*A map is like a picture of where things are or how things are arranged. If you feel that it's too hard to draw a map, draw a picture of your house and all the special places around your house where you like to play by yourself or with friends.*" If children asked, "*You mean you want a helicopter view or a bird's view?*" my response was, "*There are many different ways to draw a map. Any way you choose will be fine. Just try to figure out a way to show me your favorite places.*" Very few children had trouble with these instructions; they went to work quite readily.

I provided children with 15" by 22" paper, pencils, erasers, and an assortment of crayons. They were not allowed to use rulers. (As I have discovered before, children start to request rulers at around the age of nine.) If children spontaneously began to talk about special places, I allowed them to talk for a short time only.

When children were finished (younger children tended to finish sooner than older children), I asked them individually to tell me about the places on their maps. At the end of the interview, I asked each child to select his or her favorite place in the neighborhood. In some of the interviews, children would discuss places that they had not included on the maps. I asked fifteen of these children to create extensions of their maps, adding on another sheet of paper in the appropriate direction. This often led me to some of the children's most interesting places.

SHARED AND PRIVATE PLACES

Dens and houses occurred on children's maps or came up in interviews with 60 percent of the children. These places seem to become significant beginning around age six or seven and reach their height of importance around age ten or eleven. The children's descriptions and my observations led me to conceive of two major categories for dens— those that were primarily individual, private places and those that were the domain of a set membership of children. It appears that shared dens are important throughout later middle childhood (ages eight through eleven) but that private dens became progressively more important for children around ages ten and eleven. Many older children discussed places where they liked to *"go to be alone. It's really quiet there and I can sit all by myself."*

More recently, I have become aware of schoolyard

villages—congregations of forts that emerge on the playgrounds of some elementary schools where the staffs are open-minded. These fort villages often take on a social life of their own, with economies, established social rules, and property ownership systems. These are discussed in chapter five.

Once all the maps were completed, I sorted them into neighborhood groups to see if any places had consensus significance. In other words, did the same special places show up on several maps? Though there were numerous examples of special places that emerged in this way, I have chosen two to describe.

Buttercombe Close

Buttercombe Close is a cul-de-sac of about twenty-five single-family dwellings in a new housing development of perhaps two hundred units. In spite of the dense spacing of houses, children have access to undeveloped fields and copses adjacent to the development. Six children aged six to eleven live in this neighborhood. Five of the six included the "den in the waste place" in their maps; the other child, a six-year-old girl, mentioned it in her interview. For many of the children, it was their favorite place.

On a field trip to this area with three of the children, I found that the "waste place" was a grassy corner lot,

21

probably too small for a house, that looked intentionally set aside by the developers. The grassy area provided access to the den, a hollowed-out hedgerow on the top of a rock and dirt bank. All of the children proudly showed me their "rooms," perches in the saplings that made up the hedge, and their secret entrances. They had all worked to trim away branches in the center of the hedge. Selecting which branches would be cut was the subject of group meetings. The children also ran through the "emergency exit" procedure for me. In case intruders were coming, Becky explained, *"I line up first, Simon right behind, and Matthew. Then I run out, cross the ditch, go down the lane, and cut back through the exit into the field."* All the children exhibited a proud ownership of this den. Additionally, in an informal discussion with a mother of two of the children, she said, *"They spend all their free time there; it's really their place."*

Canada Hill

Canada Hill is a self-contained neighborhood of six single-family dwellings. The houses are about thirty years old, built along a road that leads to a pig farm. Though this area is only about a quarter mile from Buttercombe Close, the children who live here are in a separate social domain. Two children, a boy and a girl both nine years old, live on this street. Though they are rarely playmates, they share the same play area, and their maps indicate that they conceptualize this area in very similar ways. The "woods" is a brushy, overgrown thicket approximately one hundred meters long and sixty meters wide. (See figure 2-1.) Accustomed to the manicured gardens and refined landscape of south Devon, I found this to be one of the least attractive woods I'd visited. Trash littered the slopes leading down into the woods; the vegetation was thorny and scraggly. But for these two children, this patch of abandoned terrain was their haven.

Field trips with these children were conducted separately, because they were both unwilling to show their "secret dens" to each other. Alex and Kate led me through winding, often tunneled, pathways to their favorite places. Alex was specifically proud of three lookout trees, a tree that used to house a "tree den," and his current "secret den" in a dark, enclosed hollow amidst bramble. *"I don't let anyone see when I go in here,"* he confided.

Kate led me down the steps she'd helped to build, through Archie's Arch (her dog, Archie, had led her to discover this pathway through the arched tree) to the Center Roundabout. From here we went to her "Group Den," a den she created and used with a group of friends, and her "private den." She had cleaned out this area with

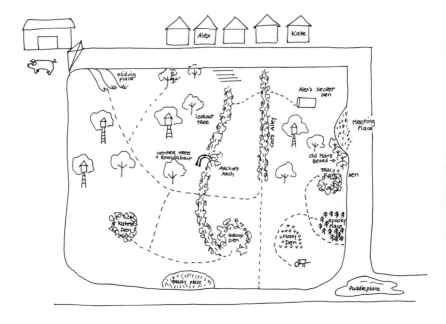

FIGURE 2-1 A composite map of the woods at Canada Hill, including excerpts from Alex's and Kate's maps and sites shown to the interviewer during field trips. Both children illustrated the woods in very similar fashion on their independently drawn maps.

24

clippers and a rake and had created a seat from three saplings. She always came here alone, to sit by herself, to clean out the den, and to read some. From another entrance point, she brought me to "Tracy and Kate's Den" and the "Mossy Den," with an old, turned-over wheelbarrow for a seat. The "woods" were laced with an ever-changing assortment of shared and private spaces, its denseness allowing for myriad privacies in a small area. As a parent, I could imagine my concern for my children playing in this area amidst rusty metal, broken glass, and casually discarded paint and aerosol cans, but it was clearly this abandoned, undefined aspect that made this space so valuable to children. Here they were free to create their own places.

PRIVATE PLACES

I visited a variety of private, personal dens with children nine to eleven years old. These places ranged from dens that were constructed with scavenged and natural materials to places that were simply found and laid claim to. Many of these places were, to my eye, remarkably innocuous. From seeing these places on children's maps, I expected isolated, clandestine hideouts. In actuality, they were often very close to home and in very public locations. But it became clear to me that in the children's eyes, these places were outposts in the wilderness. And, in fact, as children got older, these places tended to be located farther from home.

Helen's den was located approximately 20 meters from the front door to the school. A thick evergreen hedge created the boundary between one of the main roads through the village of Denbury and a residential neigh borhood. The hedge abutted a fieldstone wall, and at the juncture was a concealed entryway into the hollow hedge center. Helen described how she would sometimes stretch a piece of material over the hedge to keep out the rain, making it much cozier. And though she allowed other neighborhood children to join her on occasion, she confessed, *"Sometimes I like to stay behind after school and go there myself for a bit and not be seen."*

Nicholas's "waterbase" was located on a small island at the bend of a tiny stream. The stream was enclosed in a thicket at the bottom of steep fields. The waterbase was approximately 150 meters from home, about 50 meters beyond the edge of the housing development. One of the best aspects of this den was its limited access. Nicholas had widened the stream at the entranceway, making it difficult to hop across. He had hidden a board in the brush so that when he wanted to enter, he laid down the board, walked across, and then hid the board. He was then sealed safely inside. If he suspected interlopers, he would make a trap by covering the slow-moving water with leaves to make it look solid. Then the intruders would step on the leaves and slip into the stream. Once sealed safely inside, Nicholas could find his way into the recesses where *"no one can see you."*

Daniel, an independent eleven-year-old, took me to his den located in a copse amidst cultivated fields about 500 meters from his home. After a visit to "Monkeys Galore," a complex of well-branched trees that was the local climbers' playground, we trudged through mud and mist, across electric fences to a cluster of massive field oaks. In a cleared-out area between a fallen branch and a stone wall, Daniel had created an enclosed sitting area. "It's so quiet here, you can't hear anything but yourself." From here, he had a view over outstretched fields toward the hamlet of West Ogwell. "There's a whole landscape out there," he said with reverence. His den served both as a retreat and as a base for exploration.

THE PLAYHOUSES, PLAYSHOPS, AND BUSH HOUSES OF CARRIACOU

I planned my work with children in Carriacou to be as similar to my work in England as possible. I endeavored to find a school of similar size in a community with the same sense of cultural identity. I conducted the mapping and interviewing sessions from February through early May 1988. I visited the school two days a week and worked with groups of three or four children at a time. For a variety of reasons, I wound up working with children for two to two and a half hours rather than the shorter period of time I had used in Devon.

The second phase, field trips and expeditions, began in early March and extended through mid-May. I spent time with children after school and on Saturdays three to five days a week. I selected a representative sample of thirty-five children to work with based on the same criteria I had used in England.

The nature of the culture and my role in it caused some problems in my research:

A language barrier. Though English is the spoken and written language, the Carriacouan dialect sounds like a foreign language. Friends who visited the island would often turn to me and query, "Are they speaking English?" In the beginning, when I was struggling to understand children during interviews, I felt as though I were trying to catch fish with my hands. I could feel the shape of the words against my hands, but they kept slipping through my fingers. To overcome this problem, I started by working with older children, whose language was more accessible, and delayed working with the five- and six-year-olds until my ear was acclimated. Nonetheless, interviews with these fifteen younger children were frustrating for all of us.

The color of my skin. As a white man in a black school, I was both a novelty and an alien. I requested permission of the principal and teachers to conduct my research, and they consented, but it was clear they were somewhat ambivalent about my presence. Some teachers were interested and helpful, but others were less than enthusiastic. Their attitude was reflected in the children, though my novelty helped to outweigh this in most cases. Most children were enthusiastic in the sessions, but perhaps 25 percent gave only cursory answers to my interview questions.

The "traditional" nature of the curriculum. Teaching techniques were based on rote lecture and recitation. Children were told what to do and how to do it. The emphasis was on consuming and regurgitating set material. In contrast to Denbury, there was little or no emphasis put on personal expression or the integration of personal experience with the subject matter. As a result, my open-ended technique aimed at eliciting the expression of "special places" was disorienting for the children.

The lack of a map concept in the culture. As opposed to English children, who are exposed to Ordinance Survey maps, road maps, diagrams, and blueprints on a daily basis, Carriacouan children rarely see or use maps or diagrams. They are familiar with maps of the island and maps of the Caribbean, but these are rarely used in any personal manner, in great part because of a lack of need. As a result, children up to age eight or nine often expressed confusion about what I wanted.

VARIATION ON THE MAP-AND-INTERVIEW TECHNIQUE

The problems stated above necessitated changes in my research. Due to the open-endedness of my request, the children's reticence, and their unfamiliarity with maps, I made the following changes:

* Though the presentation of the task remained similar to the way it was presented in Devon, I introduced a discussion about maps. I asked children, *"Have you ever used a*

map? What's a map for?" Sometimes I talked about local sailors using maps to know how to avoid reefs when entering harbors, a process many were familiar with. On occasion, I drew a sample map of the school grounds. And as with the younger children in England, I encouraged them to draw pictures of their houses and favorite places if they felt they couldn't draw a map.

✳ I introduced a discussion about special places and created a list of things they might include on their maps. My objective was to make the request more explicit and less open. This list was introduced after I had worked with approximately twenty-five children. The list was developed in an attempt to make the task more like the kind of lesson they were familiar with. I presented the list during the opening discussion and then gave each child a copy of the list. During my interview, we went over the list item by item. I said, *"On your maps (or pictures) I'd like you to consider including the following places."* The list read:

Village Maps of Special Places

1. Your house
2. Roads and tracks
3. Important places—shops and friends' houses

4. Places you like to go to be alone
5. Places you like to play with friends
6. Places to explore [this was elaborated into "places you go to hunt or search for things"]
7. Places you have made on your own

❋ As the mapping and interviews proceeded, it became clear that the map was not an effective vehicle for eliciting personal responses from the children. Too often, children barely got beyond representing a few houses. Therefore, I expanded the interview component and began to interview the children while they were mapping rather than waiting until they were finished. This factor also encouraged me to begin field trips and expeditions earlier in the process. Outside of school, children were generally much more talkative and willing to share personal experiences. Field trips with children often led to experiences and places never referred to on the maps or in the interviews.

SIMILARITIES AND DIFFERENCES

Despite the problems of conducting the research, my interviews and expeditions with the children were fruitful. The clarity of the den theme in England encouraged me to focus on this issue here. On many of my field trips with children, I explicitly asked to be shown the children's found or constructed places. The more explicit interview format also turned out to be beneficial. I talked with 79 of the 101 children about these places and generated an interesting array of data. Some similarities and dissimilarities surface when comparing the English and Carriacouan children.

Similarities

* Carriacouan children illustrated the same interest in constructed and found spaces as English children. Eighty-one percent of the boys and 75 percent of the girls interviewed on this subject indicated they had built, found, or played in places like this with their friends or by themselves. In about 20 percent of the cases, children indicated these were among their favorite places.

* The height of interest in these places occurred during the eight- to eleven-year age span. This similarity is particularly interesting in light of the difference in the character of the children's maps. Carriacouan children's conceptual ability to represent space in map form was sometimes three to four years behind that of English children. In other words, some ten-year-old Carriacouan children drew maps that looked like the maps of six-year-old

33

English children. Nonetheless, there appears to be consistency in the developmental tendency toward constructed play places. This suggests a biologically programmed interest in constructed play places that unfolds on a determined schedule. On the other hand, the abstract ability to map space has to be shaped and cultivated for it to evolve in a consistent fashion. This ability occurs in a much more comprehensive manner in England than in Carriacou.

Dissimilarities

* A clearer sex role differentiation appeared in Carriacou in the kind and quality of play at constructed play places. Whereas boys referred most commonly to bush houses, often located away from home in hunting areas, girls tended to describe playhouses and playshops. This distinction was less apparent in my work with British children but has been suggested by Roger Hart.[1] (Further discussion follows.)

* There was a clear emphasis on shared places rather than private places in Carriacou. For both boys and girls, playhouses and bush houses tended to be built and used in a primarily social way. Certainly there were examples

of solitary use, but this was less clearly expressed by Carriacouan children.

DEVELOPMENTAL PATTERNS

My interviews and walks with children revealed some clear patterns. (See graphs, figure 2-2.) Boys consistently referred to their play spaces as "bush houses" rather than "playhouses" or "playshops." This suggested both a location somewhat distant from the house (though not always) and an association with being in the bush and hunting. Most notable is the intensity of interest in eight- to eleven-year-olds: 85 percent of the boys discussed bush houses, and 15 percent described playhouses. Children five to seven years old and twelve to fifteen years old were more likely to say they did not build or use these kinds of places. Most telling were two fourteen-year-old boys who said they used to build bush houses, but they did not do it anymore. One commented, "*I did that when I was nine years old.*" The tone among these older boys implied that this was "kids' stuff."

Girls were consistently interested in playhouses or playshops throughout the five to eleven year age period. They sometimes referred to the bush houses they played in

INTERVIEWS WITH 101 CHILDREN
AGED 5–15 AT HARVEY VALE SCHOOL,
CARRIACOU, GRENADA

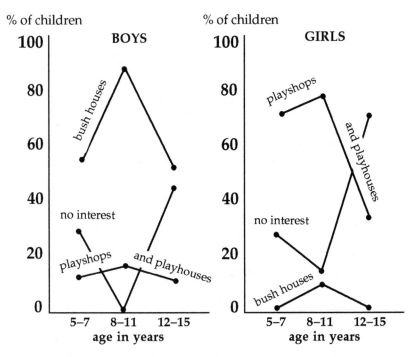

FIGURE 2-2 Children were asked to draw maps showing their favorite places and asked to show places that they had "made on their own." These places were referred to locally as "playhouses, playshops, or bush houses." The interviewer also participated in child-led field trips to favorite places. The data for each age group is a composite of the map interviews and field trips showing the prevalence of special place interest at different ages. The interest in bush houses and playhouses is greatest at ages eight through eleven and then drops off significantly at the beginning of adolescence.

with their older brothers or friends, but they expressed ownership of playhouses and shops. The eight- to eleven-year-olds showed a slightly higher percentage of interest in these places with a significant decrease in interest among the twelve- to fifteen-year-olds.

Regrettably, there were only three girls in the older group, but my interviews with them were telling. Eight- to eleven-year-old girls were consistent in their description of favorite places and activities. They liked searching for fruit in the bush, playing games in the pasture, and bathing at the beach. The older girls mentioned the Mermaid Tavern, the hotel in the main town, the historical museum, the shops, and the botanical gardens. It was clear that their focus had changed to a social context, suggesting a concurrent decrease of interest in outdoor play and construction.

UNDER THE HOUSE AND
THROUGH THE BUSH

Children up to about eight years old often described mixed boy/girl play at playshops and bush houses. It was clear this was often the imitation of adult role-play taken into an outdoor setting. *"I'll be momma, you're the baby, we go shop."* From eight to eleven, however, a differentiation started to occur. Roger Hart suggests that girls focus on the interior details of the play spaces while boys concentrate on building structures with walls and roofs.[2] While I tried not to be biased by this perspective, the distinction appeared consistent.

When I discussed this hypothesis with a British secondary schoolteacher on Carriacou, he suggested the following test. *"Tell me,"* he asked my wife and me, *"how many windows are there in your house?"* After a minute we gave him our answers, but he was uninterested. *"Tell me, where were you when you counted them?"* I described walking around the house on the outside, counting the number of storm windows that had to go on and off each year. My wife described walking from room to room inside, counting the windows, seeing the way the light poured into the rooms. The teacher said that when this experiment was attempted in a lecture hall full of 200 men and women students, most of the men counted from the outside, while most of the women counted from the inside. The yin/yang, internal/ external distinction between men and women is apparent.

In the description below, my endeavor is not to contribute to sex-role stereotyping but to suggest some of the ways in which our biologically inherited and culturally shaped roles express themselves in children's outdoor play.

PLAYHOUSES AND PLAYSHOPS

I visited the sites of eight to ten playhouses and playshops. They ranged from being clear, shady areas under tamarind trees, with few amenities, to elaborate organizations of scavenged household kitchenware and containers. Girls were "at home" in these places; they appeared nestled into and in charge of the activities here.

Valerie (age seven years, nine months) and Keisha (age eleven years, eleven months) were playing in their playhouse or "dolly house" when I arrived. Caya (age two years, six months) was sitting in Valerie's lap, and Keisha had a doll on her lap. The shade of a scraggly tamarind tree cooled an area about five meters in diameter. (Many of the local children make tamarind balls from the sweet-sour coating of the seeds of this tree.) Around the outside, defining the walls, were carefully placed branches of broom,

39

a resiny shrub used for sweeping. There were a flattened cardboard box "mattress," a three-legged chair, and a box of doll paraphernalia. The feeling was spare and a bit destitute. (The night before, Valerie, Caya, and their mother had been up all night vomiting because their cistern water was tainted. Boiling is a must during the dry season.) But the girls were proud of their space. Valerie swept it clean with broom and made sure I had a clean place to sit.

Back closer to her house was the playshop. Again, there wasn't much here. A soda container tipped on its side was the central feature. Old soft-drink cans were fitted into the slots in an orderly fashion. On top, Valerie had organized some other bottles. Later, on a walk with the girls, I realized that the house on her map was not her house but Luvisia's (a neighbor's) house. Luvisia's house was freshly painted, the walkways lined with conch shells. Valerie's house was dilapidated, with broken windows and hulks of rusting cars out front. It felt like the girls' playhouse and playshop were their means of making order in a chaotic world.

The playshop at Lorna's house was at the other end of the spectrum. Jill Brenda (age eight years, four months) described Lorna's playshop with an almost reverent, hushed tone in her voice. It was clearly her favorite place. I had come upon a playhouse built by Jill Brenda underneath one of the school buildings. Amidst a lattice of drainpipes, a roof of shredded galvanized metal protected a nestlike interior made with thick pillows of bleeding heart vine—softness in the dirt. But Lorna's playshop was really the pinnacle of embellishment. There was a clearance of no more than one meter between the floor of Lorna's wood frame house and the hard-packed but dusty ground underneath. Note taking was difficult in the cramped darkness.

As my eyes adjusted, I could see that a piece of material hung as a doorway in front of the playshop. Tops to fifty-five-gallon drums stood on end, creating the walls that enclosed an area no more than 1.5 meters square. Rocks arranged to make multiple-level shelving held a phenomenal amount of kitchenware and hardware arranged in impeccable order. On the left was a small countertop stove. On its burners rested a nest of clean frying pans and pots. The spice jars on the adjoining shelves were arranged in size order as well. Jill Brenda showed me the variety of other treasures, *"There's batteries, a nice little curtain, Christmas flowers, curlers, good, good badges* [she pinned one on], *a lock, clips, powder, pins, and a cross."* She'd barely scratched the surface. Lorna had clearly gathered and arranged things with a care and thoroughness that was compelling.

Geraldine's (age nine years, ten months) playhouse

existed mostly in her mind's eye. She took me to a spot about fifty meters from her house that she had found during a rain shower one day. A fallen tree compressed some bushes into a cavelike form on the edge of a pathway. As Geraldine sat inside waiting for me to take her picture, she absentmindedly swept the ground clean of dried leaves and arranged stones to make "a little gate." Though she didn't come here often, she said she'd like to have a little house to *"read and play by myself. I'd play cooking or put up a hammock and sleep. I'd make believe it was my real house."* When I asked her what she'd do to make it just right, she said:

It needs to be colorful, maybe some material. Yes, I'd clean it every day. Take care of it. Make a little chair and bed. If my mother would buy things, I'd make a little box for the dinette set. I'd write kitchen on one box, bedroom on another. I'd make small things as if I were a doll—except the bed. The bed would go here, and behind it a place for my duck in a little cage with food hanging from the roof above it. A wall of palm leaves next to my bed, and outside I'd cut this bush and make a little garden. I'd plant cactus around the outside so goats wouldn't go inside.

In each of these cases, there is a fascination with making things orderly and right. By putting everything in order in a small, manageable world, these girls are creating a place for themselves in the larger world.

BUSH HOUSES

I visited the sites of numerous bush houses and identified the locations of approximately twenty-five on children's maps, but I saw only two in existence. The others had all been "mashed down," either by other children or by natural processes. Additionally, the dry season is not the optimal time for building. During the rainy season, June through December, the primary building materials—leafy branches—are much more available. In any case, bush houses are clearly ephemeral, lasting for a few days to a few months. As Roger Hart suggests, the building of the structure is often more important than the actual use of the building. When I asked one boy, a good artist, to draw a bush house, he made a detailed drawing, akin to a blueprint, showing how the structure was assembled, as well as the location of nails and hinges and rope. When I asked girls to draw me pictures of playhouses or playshops, they invariably drew stereotypical house forms with shelves full of pots and pans, bottles, and foods, such as tamarind balls. Some girls could clearly describe how structures were built, and some boys were interested in interior appointments, but the tendency was as described above.

In my desire to understand bush houses better, I asked a group of boys to build one for me at a location of their choosing. This introduced an element of artifice to the situation, but as their methods matched the descriptions of other boys, I felt like I was observing an authentic process.

The spire-shaped hill of Cabesair looms over the village of Belmont like the dark promontory in *Fantasia*. Hunting for iguana and manicou (a kind of opossum) in the bush is one of the foremost activities of eight- to thirteen-year-old boys in the village. In conjunction with hunting, many of the boys build bush houses, places to go and rest while hunting or tending to their animals that are staked out to graze in high pasture areas. The boys, Randy (eight), Hollie (eleven), and Matthew (thirteen), chose a site high on the ridge between Cabesair and another unnamed hill for their bush house. (See figure 2-3.) The site chosen was in the lee of a windswept tree facing out to the northeast with a fine view.

Initially, four 2-meter-long sticks are cut with V crotches at the top. These are cut with a cutlass from flambeau and guava, known for their long, straight growth. At the site, four holes are dug in the ground with the cutlass. The ends of the poles are placed in the holes, and rocks are pounded in around the bases of the poles to make them stable. A meter-long pounding tool is cut from an

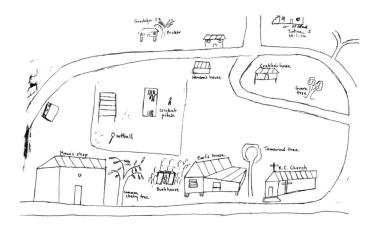

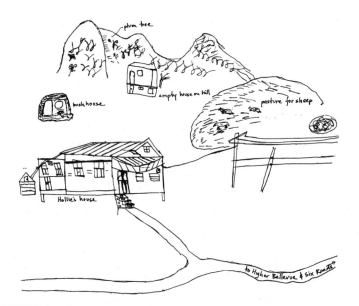

FIGURE 2-3 Excerpts from Earl's (age ten) and Hollie's (age eleven) maps of their villages, including bush houses they had constructed. Earl's was near his house; Hollie's was up in the bush.

extra pole. Horizontal poles are then placed between the uprights, resting in the V crotches at the tops of the poles. They are lashed into place with bark stripped from the poles. With this frame in place, the boys go back into the bush to cut two dozen thinner poles. They create a roof structure by crisscrossing members on the top, and they shim uprights into place to form a warp of branches for the walls. They then cut leafy branches from the canopy of bread-and-cheese and flambeau trees, lay them on the roof, and weave them into the walls. A door is framed in, and a cozy, enclosed space is created.

When I ask them what they do in bush houses, Matthew says, *"We lie down, rest ourselves, sing songs, and have nice fun. We roast corn, cook peas and sometimes birds we have trapped."* As he says this, I am reminded that children in England were always talking about how special it was to bring a picnic to their dens. It's as if food consecrates the specialness of the place, really makes the house a home of sorts. Randy also comments that he likes the bush house he made with Dane because it was all closed in so no one could see it, and it had lots of bags for sleeping on. He says it feels "warm" inside, and I sense that this is as much a feeling of security as it is a comment on the temperature.

Dwight (ten) and Nechole (eleven) both described

46

playhouses built within about fifty meters of their homes. Dwight was one of the first boys to mention spontaneously his playhouse as one of his favorite places. *"Sometimes I make a little playhouse for myself. I bring things to eat and read books."* Similarly, Nechole describes the little house he made by himself under the tamarind tree in the back garden. When I visited the site, it was occupied by a tethered pig, but it lived on in his memory. *"I wanted me to go in it, but not other people."*

SUMMARY

These last few comments serve to summarize one of the consistent elements of children's constructed and found places in both England and Carriacou. In almost all the cases cited, children expressed a need for privacy, independence, and self-sufficiency. Through making their own places, children start to carve out a place for themselves in the world. They can do it individually or through the vehicle of the peer group.

Essential to both situations, however, is the separateness from the world of parents and family. If we read Dwight's comment in a slightly modified way, I think the point becomes clear. He said, *"Sometimes I make a little playhouse for my 'self.'"*

I suspect that it is the sense of self, the ego about to be born, that is sheltered in these private places. The onset of puberty in adolescence initiates an often painful focus on "Who am I?" The construction of private places is one of the ways that children physically and symbolically prepare themselves, in middle childhood, for this significant transition.

3

FINDING A PLACE
TO DISCOVER A SELF

THE CRITICAL PERIOD
OF MIDDLE CHILDHOOD

Ever since Freud dubbed middle childhood the "latency period," many psychologists and educators have relegated it to the nether world of insignificance. If the individual is latent during this period, then it follows that no developments of great importance transpire. Early childhood is the fragile period during which the body is molded and the imagination kindled; adolescence is the fiery time when the self is forged. In between, many would have us believe, is a period of treading water. Nothing really significant happens between the change of teeth and the onset of puberty. Children learn to read and do math, but these are all quantitative changes. The really big qualitative changes happen when children stop believing in Santa Claus at six or seven years of age and when pubescent adolescents discover mirrors at age twelve or thirteen.

Major developmental shifts do occur at these ages, but we also need to focus more clearly on the middle years. Middle childhood is a critical period in the development of the self and in the individual's relationship to the natural world. By not recognizing the unique biological and psychological characteristics of the individual during this period, educators fail to provide a curriculum that is optimally attuned to the nature of the unfolding self. And it is children's interest in shaping the world, constructing small places for themselves, that gives us one of the major clues to the nature of this period.

In this chapter I elaborate on the sources of inspiration for my thinking and spell out the world-making and place-making impulses during middle childhood.

* I portray Joseph Chilton Pearce's model of development as movement through a series of matrixes, with particular emphasis on the "earth matrix" between ages seven and fourteen.

* I suggest a Jungian perspective on the relationship between the development of the self and house building and place making.

* I examine Roger Hart's speculations on place making in light of the Jungian perspective.

JOSEPH CHILTON PEARCE'S
MODEL OF DEVELOPMENT

In the past decade, Joseph Pearce has contributed a new way of understanding development in his books *Magical Child* and *Magical Child Matures*. He conceives of the child and the potential adult as having far greater psychic potential than we presently aspire to. By his account, all variety of parapsychological phenomena such as telepathy, telekinesis, astral travel, and psychic healing are available to the average person. He then lays out a portrait of the stages of development that he claims are biologically programmed to create an adult with full potential.

Pearce's views are controversial, but the appeal to me is that he has created a model of development that I have found useful. By "useful" I mean that the framework has helped me to make sense of my observations of children.

I like to think of theories as new clothes. It is important to try them on to see if they fit and feel comfortable against the skin. If they fit, if they adhere to the contours of the body, or your observations of the world, then they have proved their worth. All idea systems need to be tested this

53

way. I expect readers not to accept Pearce's ideas unquestioningly but simply to examine their usefulness in understanding children's creation of places in the world.

In *Magical Child*, Pearce contends that the individual progresses through a series of matrixes during development.[1] (See figure 3-1.) Contrary to the steplike quality of stages of development, Pearce's matrixes should be considered as a series of spheres, with the earlier matrixes contained within each subsequent one. Each matrix is the significant world, or the safe place in which the individual resides. Therefore, the individual is at home in, or gets his or her strength from, the matrixes in the following sequence:

> WOMB MATRIX: conception to birth
> MOTHER/FAMILY MATRIX: birth through seven years
> EARTH MATRIX: seven through fourteen years
> SELF MATRIX: fourteen through twenty-one years
> MIND-BRAIN MATRIX: twenty-one through twenty-eight years
> MIND MATRIX: twenty-eight years and beyond

Each matrix provides the individual a safe place within which to reside, a source of energy, and a place from which to explore out into the world, most specifically into the subsequent matrix.

PEARCE'S MATRIXES
OF HUMAN DEVELOPMENT

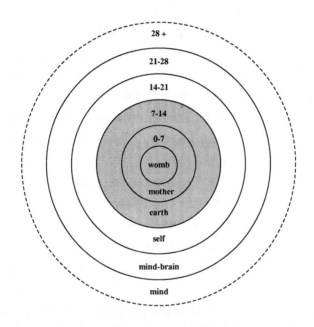

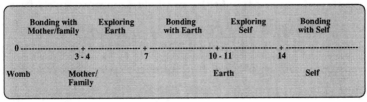

FIGURE 3-1

55

The eighteen-month-old child in an unfamiliar situation provides a concrete model of the general pattern. At eighteen months, the child is supported within the mother/family matrix. Obviously, the mother and family provide all the child's physical and psychological needs and encourage her or him to interact with the world. On the beach, my eighteen-month-old daughter makes small exploratory forays away from our beach towel. She ambles down to the water's edge, splashes about, and then heads back after a few minutes for a hug. She gambols down the beach, crouching to pick up a shell, look at a crab, or watch diving pelicans, and then loops back to sit with her mother. This pattern of gradually increasing explorations with returns to home base for reassurance is the basic exploratory pattern of early childhood.

Pearce contends that if development proceeds as biologically programmed, each matrix provides this kind of safe retreat, the known amidst the unknown. Each movement from one matrix to the next is like a new birth, but the process of exploration ensures that there are bridges from one to the next. Each matrix is a safe place to return to and a jumping-off point for discovering new aspects of personal development.

The child spends the first three to four years of life establishing a firm relationship with the mother/family matrix. At around four years old, the well-bonded child begins to actively explore the earth matrix. He or she becomes interested, for example, in how roads fit together or in finding out where animals live. Children start to get lost at this age because they wander off, intrigued to find out where the kitty is going. By age seven, children feel comfortable enough in the natural and social worlds to differentiate themselves from the family and step into the earth matrix. They start to make a home for themselves in the natural world. Children's neighborhood maps show a significant change around this age. Up to age seven, the family house is drawn quite large and usually in the center of the map. After this age, the size of the house decreases rapidly, the family home moves to the periphery of the map, and the landscape of the neighborhood takes center stage.

Children then spend the next four years creating a relationship with the earth matrix—they bond with the earth, or at least that's what they are supposed to do. By age eleven, they feel at home in the earth matrix, grounded in the natural world, and they begin to explore the self matrix. By age fourteen, they make the transition out of the earth matrix and into the self matrix.

A wide range of developmentalists and social institutions have identified the significant shift that begins around age six or seven. Piaget talks about the beginning of concrete operations, Erikson talks about the advent of autonomy, the Catholic church contends that from this point on the individual is capable of sin. Until only recently, this has been the traditional school-entering age. All these developmental models suggest that from this point on, the child has an individuated life.

The unquenchable appetite for the out-of-doors that many children show at this age is an indicator of the move into the earth matrix. Pearce's use of the term "earth matrix" refers broadly to the actual stuff of the concrete world—trees, dirt, animals, and plants of the natural world, as well as pencils, houses, clothes, and the humanmade things of the world. As Piaget contends that appropriate learning is through the actual stuff of the world, Pearce contends that it is in this world that children start to feel at home.

In an attempt to understand this progression in my own life, I have sifted through my memories to choose one significant memory from each year of my life between ages four and nine. Relating a few of these makes this transition clear.

At *four*, my memory is of digging in the sand box right outside the kitchen window. I know my mother is inside within hearing distance. I dig as deep as I can, put my ear to the ground, and I can faintly hear the tinkly sound of bells mounted on bike handlebars. In my mind, I see thousands of people in upside-down funnel-shaped hats riding bicycles through city streets. I know that I have dug far enough so that I can hear the sounds of China on the other side of the earth.

At *five*, I remember the dark, lonely walk to the bus stop. I am in kindergarten and feel nervous every day I leave home to make the trek. The bus stop is separated from a swamp by a rock wall. I am always looking over my shoulder while I am there because the older children have said that snapping turtles will come out of the swamp, creep over the wall, and bite you when you're not looking. I don't like having to go so far from my home on my own.

At *six*, Heidi and I, both first graders, shun games of "Red Rover" and "Red Light, Green Light." Instead we go off to an isolated area at the edge of the playground. We stand on a tree stump, jump off, and will ourselves to fly. I am sure that when I will myself to fly, I stay in the air about half a second longer than when I don't try. I do this every day for a long time. We call it playing fairies. I know that there's something weird about this, so I never tell anyone about it.

At *seven*, I always want to spend my Saturdays at the stream coming out of the mill pond about a half mile from my home. Here I build dams of mud, leaves, and sticks, and then build elaborate villages downstream complete with houses, docks, boardwalks, bridges, and causeways. I choose where I might have lived, how I might escape. Then I tear a break in the dam and watch the structures all get washed downstream.

At *nine*, Kevin and I spend a series of days throughout one autumn making forays into the forbidden fields and forests beyond his house. Each time we go a little farther. Our goal is an abandoned water tower with miles of ladders up the inside to a tiny platform. Making it to this platform is a joy beyond believing, the realization of a wild dream.

This series of memories is illustrative of the move out of the mother/family matrix into the earth matrix. At four, I need to be within earshot of my mother for my sense of security. By nine, I have a thirst to explore the corners of the surrounding landscape and spend much of my free time in such pursuits. I am beginning to be at home in the earth matrix.

Annie Dillard describes this same kind of questing into the urban landscape of Pittsburgh when she was nine years old:

Walking was my project before reading. The text I read was the town; the book I made up was a map. First I had walked across one of our side yards to the blackened alley with its buried dime. Now I walked to piano lessons, four long blocks north of school and three zigzag blocks into an Irish neighborhood near Thomas Boulevard.

I pushed at my map's edges. Alone at night I added newly memorized streets and blocks to old streets and blocks, and imagined connecting them on foot. On darkening evenings I came home exultant, secretive, often from some exotic leafy curb a mile beyond what I had known at lunch, where I had peered up at the street sign, hugging the cold pole, and fixed the intersection in my mind. What joy, what relief, eased me as I pushed open the heavy front door!—joy and relief because, from the trackless waste, I had located home, family and the dinner table once again.[2]

In order to go farther and farther in their explorations, many children create an outpost, a place to be "at home" in the out-of-doors. Herein lies one psychological component of why children find and build houses, forts, and dens. As they start to sense their independence from parents, they start to feel a need to have a separate space. Younger children do this in the form of blankets over tables, the space underneath the stairwell, the wardrobe in the attic. But starting around seven, children want these places to be outside the house, both as a way of separating from parents and because they want to be in the natural world.

First houses in the out-of-doors are often under the porch or under a tree adjacent to the house. Children in Carriacou often set up in the space underneath the house or in an unused chicken coop close by. Children in England often choose hedge-den locations at the perimeters of their yards. But as children progress to ages nine to eleven, the move is to isolated tree dens or bush houses, places out of sight of parents and the social milieu.

It is significant that the height of interest in dens and bush houses is in this nine to eleven age frame. This is the bonding phase of Pearce's earth matrix, and the results of my research with children in England and Carriacou resonate with this model. If Pearce is right about the process of bonding with the earth matrix, then one would predict that this middle age range would be the time of maximum interest in homes in the out-of-doors. Then, as children start to become more preoccupied with notions of self and performance within the social context, one would expect a decrease in this kind of activity.

This was borne out on the last day of my research in Carriacou. Children started to express a lack of interest in playhouses and bush houses around the age of twelve. In place of that interest, I discovered a new phenomenon. Claigon had told me that he was building a bush house, and I had been after him to show it to me. On my last day in school, I asked him about it. *"I not building a bush house anymore, I building a board house behind me house."* When I went to investigate, I found a new phase of place making in the works. Three boys, Matthew (thirteen), Claigon (fourteen), and Shane (twelve) were all building board houses. As opposed to bush houses, which were made from native materials and located in isolated spots, these structures were made from scavenged building timber and materials and located within twenty meters of the boys' houses. They were essentially minihouses, built along the model of existing homes with frame construction, accurate measurements, diagonal bracing, and proper doors and windows. When I asked Claigon why he had abandoned the bush house in favor of the board house, he replied, *"Going to the bush is too much trouble, and here I could come and bring friends, play cards."* When I asked about keeping others out he said, "No, I want to bring friends in." He also revealed that there was a kind of informal competition going on to see who among the three of them could build the best house.

In Pearce's terms, these boys were exploring the social concerns and issues in anticipation of the move out of the earth matrix into the self matrix. The boys were testing their skills against each other and using these spaces for card playing, distinctly in imitation of adult social gatherings.

Therefore, the nature of the structures that children choose to build reflects their current developmental issues and interests.

A JUNGIAN PERSPECTIVE ON HOUSE BUILDING AND PLACE MAKING

As opposed to Freud's emphasis on sexuality and its repression in his characterization of stages of development, Jung's major emphasis was on the individuation of the self as the motive force in development. I have no aspirations to synopsize Jung's model. Instead, I want to focus on some memories from Jung's autobiography relating to the development of his sense of self and apply them to understanding children's house-building and place-making tendencies.

Jung's remarkable ability to access the quality and content of childhood thinking provides us with an unusual portrait of the psychological and philosophical musings of children. Though children in middle childhood often have deeply moving ideas about their place in the world, they often do not have the ability to express these ideas. This inability does not deny the experience. Jung's recollections allow us to grasp these often inexpressible sensations.

Starting around eight years old, Jung was attracted to

the cavelike nooks and crannies of a large stone wall bordering a garden. He recalls,

I used to tend a little fire in one of these caves, . . . a fire that had to burn forever and therefore had to be constantly maintained by our united efforts. No one but myself was allowed to tend this fire. . . . My fire alone was living and had an unmistakable aura of sanctity.

Consider, perhaps, that the fire within this protected space is a symbol of Jung's emerging self. Soon after this period, he recalls a recurrent experience that takes this notion a step further:

In front of this wall was a slope in which was embedded a stone that jutted out—my stone. Often, when I was alone, I sat on this stone, and then began an imaginary game that went something like this: "I am sitting on top of this stone and it is underneath." But the stone also could say "I" and think: "I am lying here on this slope and he is sitting on top of me." The question then arose: "Am I the one who is sitting on top of the stone, or am I the stone on which he is sitting?" This question always perplexed me, and I would stand up, wondering who was what now.

At this point in his development, Jung's sense of self was not yet differentiated, the "I" was labile, located sometimes within his body and sometimes within the rock. Jung then continues:

65

What this meant was revealed soon afterward, in my tenth year. My disunion with myself and uncertainty in the world at large led me to an action which at the time was quite incomprehensible to me.

Jung describes how he created a carved male figurine. He painted the figure, made a little coat for it, and placed it in a little bed in his pencil box. In the case, he placed a smooth, black stone—"this was his stone." He then hid the pencil box on the rafters in his attic, in a place that he was sure no one would ever find. He returned regularly to unwrap and inspect his little man, making sure he was still there, and then hide him again.

I contented myself with the feeling of newly won security, and was satisfied to possess something that no one knew and no one could get at. . . . I felt safe and the tormenting sense of being at odds with myself was gone. In all difficult situations, whenever I had done something wrong or my feelings had been hurt, or when my father's irritability or my mother's invalidism oppressed me, I thought of my carefully bedded-down and wrapped-up manikin and his smooth prettily colored stone.

The absolute seclusion of this hidden figure was crucial for Jung at this point in his development.

Finally, Jung describes an experience that occurred two years later as he was walking to school one day:

Suddenly for a single moment I had the overwhelming impression of having just emerged from a dense cloud. I knew all at once: now I am myself! It was as if a wall of mist were at my back, and behind that wall there was not yet an "I." But at this moment I came upon myself. Previously I had existed, too, but everything had merely happened to me. Now I happened to myself. . . . Previously I had been willed to do this and that; now I willed. This experience seemed to me tremendously important and new: there was "authority" in me. Curiously enough, at this time . . . I had lost all memory of the treasure in the attic. Otherwise I would probably have realized even then the analogy between my feeling of authority and the feeling of value which the treasure inspired.[3]

This sequence of experiences from tending a fire, musing on the rock, shaping the secret manikin, and then emerging into a sense of self is a portrait of the emergence of the consciousness of self as unique and distinct between the ages of eight and twelve. There is a progression from sensing the vibrant energy of the soul within the fire, to musing on the locus of the self, to creating a concrete image of the self in the form of the little man, to coming upon the abstract sense of self within. Pearce might describe this as making forays into the self matrix.

Compare Jung's need for a sense of secrecy around age

ten with the following excerpt from a poem written by a
ten-year-old girl. Upon hearing of my interest in children's
landscape experiences, a colleague of mine described his
writing work with fifth-grade children. Quite independent of my work, he had found that asking children to
write about their "special places" was one of the best ways
to elicit closely descriptive prose. About half of the pieces
described forts and hideouts. One poem starts this way:

A special place is in the woods very far away.
It is in the biggest oak tree I ever saw.
It is about eight feet off the ground.

All you could hear is birds and other peaceful sounds.
Before I climb I carve the words DO NOT DISTURB.
It takes a long time to climb.
There are steps to help you.
No one or nobody knows where this is,
not even my brothers. . . .

I don't have a secret password because
no one knows where it is.
If you tried to find it you could not because
there are branches covering it.

And consider the similarity of this poem about a secret
place written by Edith Chase, a woman in her seventies
remembering being ten years old:

When the first thin light comes creeping,
  Up the early edge of day,
And the household still is sleeping,
  Then I dress and slip away
To the place that I am keeping
  For my secret hideaway.

Stealing toward the giant billow
  Of a tree across the lawn
Like a leafy mammoth pillow,
  In the dim delight of dawn
Up I climb into my willow
  While the night is hardly gone.

Up in the willow is wispy and whispery,
Silent and silvery, misty with mystery.

Nobody else in the world is awake!
Nobody knows how the little leaves quake.
Nobody knows that the willow is mine.
Nobody knows of my shadowy shrine.
Nobody knows of the place where I hide
My notebook and stub of a pencil inside
My mystery box of waterproof tin.

Nobody knows I am writing in
The favorite thoughts and the singing rhymes
That I think to myself and write sometimes.

Nobody knows of my special tree
Where we are alone, my secret and me.[4]

During this period of middle childhood, the self is fragile and under construction and needs to be protected from view of the outside world. The secretive nature of the hiding place is significant. The self, like the metamorphosing larva of the butterfly, needs to be wrapped in a cocoon before it emerges into the light. Thus, the places that children seek out are places where they cannot be seen, places to begin the unfolding of the self.

Clare Cooper Marcus, in her exploratory essay "The House as a Symbol of the Self," maps out a Jungian way of thinking about the relationship between our houses and our sense of self.[5] At about the age of fifty, Jung began the process of building himself a house. Over the next twenty-five years, he constructed a complex house that had begun as a simple round house. At new stages in his life, he added new components to reflect new concerns and needs. In reflecting on the process, Jung describes,

From the beginning I felt the tower as in some way a place of maturation—a maternal womb or a maternal figure in which I could become what I was, what I am and will be. It gave me a feeling as if I were being reborn in stone. It is thus a concretization of the individuation process. During the building work, of course, I never considered these matters. I built the house in sections, always following the concrete needs of the moment. It might also be said that I built it in a kind of dream. Only afterward did I see how all the parts fitted together and that a meaningful form had resulted: a picture of psychic wholeness.[6]

Cooper Marcus suggests that in considering Jung's reflections, *"we are not just examining one man's inner life; hopefully, there is something here of the inner symbolism of all men."*[7] I wish to stretch the notion even more and contend there is also truth in this for children. Children's house building and place finding can be seen in this light as the "roughing in" of the self. First, a simple feeling of specialness is found in the landscape. Then branches are piled together or a few boards lashed together to create a primitive structure. Eventually, the interior is modified, a rug installed, shelves built. Progressively, a unique space is shaped that reflects the emerging self. Thus, children's building activities are also "a concretization of the individuation process." Because children need to interact with concrete materials to ground the thinking process in middle childhood, they need to use wood, stone, and earth to engage in the process of letting the self be born.

Merging these two sets of memories from Jung's life, we come up with a suggestive model for understanding children's house building and place finding. As Jung needed to sequester his man in the dark attic where it would not be found, children create spaces in which they "cannot be seen." In these places, children have experiences that are not shared in the broad, adult, or social milieu. The experience of finding a place that is "just for me" or that "I built all by myself" transmutes into a sense of personal uniqueness. The special place outside serves to symbolize the special person inside.

ROGER HART'S REFLECTIONS ON FORTS AND HOUSES

Roger Hart's landmark study of the children of Wilmington, Vermont, supports this Jungian perspective. Over a period of two years, Hart studied the experience of place of eighty-four school-age children. In this work, Hart makes it clear through quantitative analysis of his interviews and explorations with the children that forts and houses ranked third in terms of children's place preferences. In speculating on why these places were so important, he is critical of Freud's suggestion that these are simply indicative of a regressive tendency to return to the womb. Instead he suggests, *"These places serve excellently as places of retreat to look at the world from a place of one's own, as places for experimenting with how to put things together and locales for hide and seek."* Further, he suggests these places are valuable in that they provide *"the satisfaction of being able to transform the environment successfully and comfort in being able to make a place for oneself—ordering the world assists in the development of a sense of personal order."* Although I am essentially in agreement, I wish to take the notion a step further by stressing the affective component of house building. Not only does the place help in creating personal order, it is actually one of the vehicles by which the self is shaped.

One of Hart's family studies includes an illustrative quote from seven-year-old David, who says, *"Some day I want to make a tree fort and tell no one and I'll keep it locked. We're making a fort, but there's only one side up. I feel like it's all my own. When I make snow forts with Annie and Jo, I feel like it's all mine—like I want to just have it all my own."*

This comment illustrates the intense significance of personal ownership and secrecy. In a previous passage, Hart comments on the reason places are often called forts. He suggests that this name must have been "passed down within boys' subculture, because I saw no use of forts as places for defense." The problem is that Hart interprets this term literally. Certainly, the cavalry's romantic history in conquering the Wild West left us a legacy of forts that live on in boys' imaginations, but there is a deeper reason the name has caught on. David's comments above suggest the fort is a place he wants to be sacrosanct and defended. He wants to be able to lock it to protect it from the rest of the world. He and other children have made it clear that intruders are not welcome, that the location is often secret so others will not find out.

These places are called forts because they serve as retreats from the forces of the world. As the notion of the self starts to mature in middle childhood, children start to perceive how fragile their individuality is in face of the big world outside. The small, manageable world of the fort, with everything pulled inside, is calm and reassuring. It provides a protective barrier within which personal forces can be summoned to deal with the onslaught of otherness. This Jungian perspective serves to take Hart's findings to another level of psychological significance. As Hart says in his recollections of his own childhood landscapes, *"The most important quality of these areas was that they were our own."* We need to recognize and respect children's need to find a place of their own as a step toward becoming their own persons.

4

TRY TO REMEMBER

AN HOMAGE TO EDITH COBB

When I first read Edith Cobb's "The Ecology of Imagination in Childhood," I got tingles up and down my spine. I felt it had been written just for me. This article was first published in *Daedalus* in 1959 but was popularized by inclusion in *The Subversive Science* in 1969.[1] Over the years I've returned to it over and over again, like a *Rocky Horror Picture Show* enthusiast. I cheer at the same parts, get inspired anew by the ideas. "You've got to read this!" I've said to dozens of students and colleagues.

Recently there has been an Edith Cobb revival. Her book, which bears the same title as the article, came back in print for a while, and there has been an upsurge in the number of times she is referenced in professional journals. In fact, the passages cited below are almost becoming overused in the field of environmental psychology, but they are the organic soil in which many of my ideas have flourished. I am indebted to her insights.

In this chapter I examine adults' memories of forts and other special places. After an overview of Cobb's insights and an analytical critique of her work, I present adults' memories of finding and building special places. This includes both a sense of the significance of the experience at the time and the long-term effect on the adult personality of these childhood experiences.

Edith Cobb points to middle childhood as a unique stage in development for the fostering of the relationship between the person and the natural world:

My position is based upon the fact that the study of the child in nature, culture and society reveals that there is a special period, the little understood, prepubertal, halcyon, middle age of childhood, approximately from five or six to eleven or twelve, between the strivings of animal infancy and the storms of adolescence—when the natural world is experienced in some highly evocative way, producing in the child a sense of some profound continuity with natural processes.[2]

The notion of the "critical period" in biological development emerged after Cobb's work. But in this statement, she is suggesting that certain kinds of experience need to occur during this middle childhood time frame in order to ensure healthy psychological development.

The "critical period" notion is well developed in the fields of animal behavior and language development. If the white-throated sparrow chick is not exposed to the correct song of its species during a certain prescribed period (between one month and two months of age), it will not develop a normal song. In other words, certain kinds of learning need to happen at very specific times in the individual's life. The assumption is that this requirement is genetically programmed.

Language learning in humans has similar characteristics, though the critical period is much broader. There appears to be a highly sensitive language-learning period between six months and six years. It is broadly recognized that children can learn multiple languages during these years. I had a friend whose four-year-old could speak three languages after having grown up in the Philippines where her father spoke English, her mother Spanish, and the housekeeper a local dialect. Similarly, persistent hearing problems during these years can lead to permanent, long-term speech problems.

There is a secondary period of language-learning sensitivity from age six to puberty. It is commonly accepted that after puberty and into adulthood the language-learning capacity diminishes. Clearly, the human organism is programmed for language learning during a certain phase of development. (It's a discouraging commentary on public education that second language instruction in the United

States usually begins at age twelve, precisely at the time when the sensitivity to language learning is ending. This is a prime example of education not in synchronization with development.)

What is critical about this middle childhood age period? What kinds of experiences are crucial for children during these years? If we can determine the answers to these questions, then we have the basis for reconceptualizing elementary education.

Certainly Piaget has pointed us toward a recognition of the need for involvement with concrete materials during this stage of "concrete operational thinking." Children are biologically programmed to learn and create concepts through working with things, rather than just ingesting words and symbols. Some contend that if children don't experience this kind of education, they are often hampered throughout life. But Edith Cobb points us in some new directions for considering the kinds of involvement that are important for children during this period:

The genius of childhood, in the sense of extreme personal originality and the creation of private worlds, is discontinuous and persists into adult life only as a specialized, highly cultivated condition.

From her extensive observations and psychological testing of children, she claims:

I became acutely aware that what a child wanted to do most of all was to make a world in which to find a place to discover a self. This ordering reverses the general position that self-exploration produces a knowledge of the world. Furthermore, while observing the passionate world-making behavior of the child when he is given plastic materials and working dimensions which are manageable and in proportion to his need . . . I have been made keenly aware of those processes which the genius in particular in later life seeks to recall.[3]

Cobb is suggesting that what is crucial is the opportunity to participate in world-making or world-shaping activities. Children need the opportunity to create, within prescribed limits, small worlds. The creation of these worlds from shapable, open-ended materials such as sand, wood, clay, and Legos, gives children the opportunity to organize a world and then find places in which they can become themselves. The following descriptions of dollhouse play from the ages of six and seven illustrate the power of this kind of self-contained, shapable world.

Rosanne McCarthy, age thirty-eight, recalls her memories of playing with a dollhouse in a cousin's house that she visited irregularly:

The adults are all talking about stuff I don't care about and I want to go downstairs to the dollhouse. For the first time they let me go down cellar by myself. It's dark and smells musty as I go toward the back of the cellar where the stairway light barely reaches. I'm cautious and afraid of getting lost. I know it's in a little room off to the side, but I don't want any adults down here with me. I wave my hand around in the gloom trying to locate the light switch. . . . Got it!

There it is! It's always as beautiful as I imagine. Everything around the dollhouse is blurred in my memory; just the house stands out. Inside there are pictures on the wall, chandeliers that light, and tiny furniture with drawers that open. The first thing I want to do is turn on the lights in the miniature rooms. It's almost a ceremony. I pause, enjoying the anticipation. I throw the switch; the glow is delightful!

Tiny shadows are thrown on the floor and the walls. The furniture is so delicate that I'm afraid of breaking it. Just touching it gives me shivers. But I want to touch it, change it, rearrange the furniture. I'm lost in play; time has no meaning. It's my world to change any way I like, to manipulate to whatever plot I want. I'm speaking aloud quietly to myself. I'm there winding down the stairs, going from room to room, arranging things so they are pleasing to me. I'm insulated from the adults upstairs—from the whole world, for that matter.[4]

Cathy Sprague, age twenty-nine, recalls a dollhouse experience from the same age period. These reflections were written separately, with no discussion between the authors. In this light, the parallels are striking:

What was it like to play in my dollhouse? It was a little like being a big person. I could put words in the dad's mouth and the mom's. I could go off to work, stay home and cook, worry about the baby. If I wanted to, I could leave the house altogether, as one of the dolls, and take the dog for a walk. I could play for hours, talking for all the characters in my little girl's voice, totally in control of my world. [5]

Clearly, being master of the dollhouse was an empowering experience for these girls. As Cobb suggests, dollhouses "have working dimensions which are manageable and are in proportion" to these girls' needs. The confined space and scope allow the girls to project themselves into this world and make it their own. They become the authors of their own experience. Thus, small-world experience in childhood roughs in the ego's early sense of productive shaping of the world; it is the groundwork for taking an active role later in life.

These reflections by adults on childhood experiences bring us to another important element of Cobb's work. One of the unusual contributions of her work was her survey of the autobiographies of genius:

In my collection of some three hundred volumes of autobiographical recollections of their own childhood by creative thinkers from many cultures and eras, it is principally to this middle-age range in their early life that these writers say they return in memory in order to renew the power and impulse to create at its very source, a source which they describe as the experience of emerging not only into the light of consciousness but into a living sense of a dynamic relationship with the outer world. In these memories the child appears to experience a sense of discontinuity, an awareness of his own unique separateness and identity, and also a continuity, a renewal of relationship with nature as process.[6]

In these moments, children have the experience of being simultaneously immersed in *and* separate from the environment.

Cobb's hypothesis has been refreshingly researched and critiqued by Louise Chawla. After examining this critique I present my findings of adults' memories of place-making experiences. I am interested in what adults can tell us about why they engaged in making and finding special places and how such activities affect their adult views of the world.

CHAWLA'S CRITIQUE OF EDITH COBB

The one serious evaluation of Edith Cobb's hypotheses has been accomplished by Louise Chawla in her papers entitled "Ecstatic Places" and "The Ecology of Environmental Memory." Chawla sets out to *"test the theory of*

Edith Cobb that adult creativity is directly built upon a childhood sense of self and world."[7] To test this hypothesis, Chawla surveyed thirty-eight autobiographies of twentieth-century Americans, consciously chosen because they were different from the predominantly eighteenth- and nineteenth-century European autobiographies that Cobb surveyed. She then evaluated the "universality" of the transcendent experience with nature in middle childhood that Cobb pointed to. Did all autobiographers refer to these kinds of experiences? Chawla then sought to explore whether the autobiographers specifically used these experiences to inspire their adult thinking.

Chawla found that Cobb's transcendent, ecstatic experience was not universally reported in the autobiographies. However, fifteen of her thirty-eight autobiographers did relate striking environmental encounters. Furthermore, although only a few cited these experiences as inspiration for adult work, many of them indicated that their experiences served as *"a reservoir of calm and strength within the self."* She cites an autobiography by Howard Thurman, a minister and author:

When the storms blew, the branches of the large oak tree in our backyard would snap and fall. But the topmost branches of the oak tree would sway, giving way just enough to save themselves from snapping loose. I needed the strength of that tree, and like it,

I wanted to hold my ground. Eventually, I discovered that the oak tree and I had a unique relationship. I could sit, my back against its trunk, and feel the same peace that would come to me in bed at night. I could reach down in the quiet places of my spirit, take out my bruises and my joys, unfold them and talk about them. I could talk aloud to the oak tree and know that I was understood. It, too, was a part of my reality, like the woods, the night, and the pounding surf, my earliest companions, giving me space. [8]

This and other passages suggest a broad tendency, if not a universal experience, for children to find or make special places during middle childhood that hold special meaning throughout their lives; they become places of repose, of sureness, to return to. My discussions and interviews with adults confirm this.

ADULT MEMORIES

A fascinating study of religious experience in childhood provides a thought-provoking starting point for these reflections. Edward Robinson, in *The Original Vision*, presents remembrances of life-changing experiences solicited randomly from adults throughout the British Isles. [9] He contends, in his analysis of this study, that contrary to our assumption that religious experience starts only at adolescence, many children between the ages of three and twelve have moving religious experiences that they are not able to describe until much later in their lives. In defending the validity of these remembered experiences from criticisms that the memories have been shaped by later adult experience, Robinson says:

Childhood can not be fully understood simply by the observation of children. Quite apart from the difficulties of communication in the pre-adolescent years, there is often a dimension to our early experiences that we can only become fully conscious of (if at all) in later life, when we compare them with other forms of experience that lack that dimension; in childhood we may be wiser than we know.

Children's descriptions of experiences are a valuable source of insight, but adults' memories can put childhood experience into a valuable context.

In a chapter on nature mysticism, Robinson relates the following description offered by a fifty-seven-year-old woman:

The most profound experience of my life came to me when I was very young—between four and five years old. . . . My mother and I were walking on a stretch of land in Pangbourne Berks, known locally as "the moors." As the sun declined and the slight chill of evening came on, a pearly mist formed over the ground. . . . Suddenly, I seemed to see the mist as a shimmering gossamer tissue and the harebells, appearing here and there, seemed to shine with a brilliant fire. Somehow I understood that this was the living tissue of life itself, in which that which we call consciousness was embedded, appearing here and there as a shining focus of energy in the more diffused whole. In that moment I knew that I had my own special place, as had all other things, animate and so-called inanimate, and that we were all part of this universal tissue which was both fragile yet immensely strong, and utterly good and beneficent.

The vision has never left me. It is as clear today as fifty years ago, and with the same intense feeling of love of the world and the certainty of ultimate good. . . . The whole of this experience has ever since formed a kind of reservoir of strength fed from an unseen source. Of course, at the early age of four or five I could not have expressed anything of the experience in the words I have now used, and perhaps the attempt to convey the absorption of myself into the whole. . . . But the point is that, by whatever mysterious perception, the whole impression and its total meaning were apprehended in a single instant.[10]

This is a clear illustration of exactly the kind of experience Edith Cobb posits as universal and that Louise Chawla found to occur only in some autobiographers' recollections. This child clearly felt simultaneously merged with the world (*"we were all part of this universal tissue"*) and separate and distinct from the world (*"I knew I had my own special place"*). But my main point in presenting the experience here is to lend credence to the notion that adult recollections can flesh out the significance of a childhood experience beyond observations and explanations of children.

ESCAPE BEHIND THE BILLBOARDS: URBAN VS. RURAL FORTS

Numerous examples of forts and special places can be found from children living in rural areas. The access to open space and parents' greater sense of safeness provides children with the protection and freedom they need to feel comfortable to explore and create places. Many authors have commented on the restrictedness of urban environments in terms of providing free opportunities for children. Lisa Murrow wrote in the *City Childhood Newsletter*,

In the city, children may construct a fort—if it doesn't interfere with an adult's use of space, if the child finds an empty corner. . . . The thrill of learning to walk down a dirt road to see a friend is replaced by the child's (and the parents') fears about traffic and strangers as he or she takes longer excursions on city sidewalks and streets. Seeing our children relax, run and play with such total abandon when they reach the ocean [the

Murrows were living near the ocean in the Santa Monica district of Los Angeles] *makes us realize how starved they are for a landscape which they can change and shape until it is part of their play. They need spaces which are theirs alone.* [11]

Though I agree with Murrow's contention, I have found that children's drive to create private spaces is so deep that many urban children find opportunities despite all the obstacles. As I found amongst children in Devon, quite small and innocuous spaces can meet children's needs. My wife, for instance, who grew up in Santa Monica, used the dry canyon bottoms that sliced through urban and suburban developments as the place to play Robinson Crusoe when she was ten or eleven. She and a friend would set up a camp and then explore from there for the necessities to provision themselves on their imagined desert island. Urban children are skilled at discovering interstitial spaces, the spaces between other areas with designated functions. Certainly city parks are extremely valuable, but culverts, alleyways, basements, abandoned warehouses, railroad right-of-ways, and hedges are all utilized. Sally Middlebrooks' research with children in East Harlem identifies some children's proclivity to use these spaces for place making.

From the many adult memories I have collected through questionnaires and papers written by graduate students at Antioch New England Graduate School and from interviews with teachers and parents in New England, Devon, England, and Carriacou, Grenada, I offer one urban, one suburban, and one rural example. I include these to show how the place-making impulse exerts itself in nonnatural settings and how the experience is similar regardless of the nature of the environment. These accounts do not stand alone but are merely representative of many similar descriptions.

The following description was written by Bonnie Baron, age twenty-eight, recalling a special place in urban New Jersey experienced when she was eight and nine years old:

Walking along the sidewalks, cluttered with broken toys, bikes, and baby carriages, there was always a feeling of anticipation in our chests when we had our special destination in mind. Weighted down by our bouncing, gurgling canteens, we would soon cross the street and proceed down the long, uneven alleyway, always gathering a stone or two in our sneakers. Our pace quickened as we turned and approached the waist-high field of weeds and grasses. We felt totally camouflaged in the network of green. If we fell, would we be submerged beneath the sea of green?

Now our eyes focused on the two slanted billboards ahead. We never noticed what was posted on their fronts as we chose to remain behind them in our world of gray privacy. Was there a sidewalk and a street on the other side? I suppose so. But we were content staying behind the billboards and being shielded from the noise, traffic, and clamor.

Phew! We were finally there. The cool shade dried the sweat from our foreheads. Had anyone discovered our secret place while

91

we were away? No. Everything seemed in place as we had left it. "Let's get the flag out," I whispered to Ann. We always spoke quietly in case someone might be listening from across the traffic-laden street. Uncovering the flag and securing it to the ground made our presence seem officially declared.

We were busy from the moment we arrived. We made cabinets as painstakingly as master carpenters with two slabs of uneven, discarded wood—a perfect display area for our utensils of sticks, rocks, and branches. Digging holes for hiding special treasures occupied much of our time, even though we used our stick and rock tools with precision and speed. Also, we were mathematicians of the highest degree with our twigs for calculating the number of trucks that rolled by.

Oh no! I hear someone coming. Quick—sneak down into the grasses. Surely we will not be seen. We hope the pounding of our hearts will not be heard. STOMP. STOMP. STOMP. Away the intruders go. Safe again!

Time to put everything away for the day. As we tug the flag out of the ground, our special world ends for the afternoon.[12]

Suburban areas are sometimes more devoid of appropriate play spaces than urban areas because of the paucity of interstitial space. Because expansive housing developments are completely planned, no undefined areas are left that allow children to play with natural materials. In the face of this homogenized environment, suburban children often need to turn inward to find a suitable place to call their own. Nancy Segreto, age twenty-eight, describes her solution:

As long as I could remember, our unfinished basement was one huge playroom. In a dark corner of the basement, where we hardly ever played, there was a small, black opening high up in the wall. At around the age of eight, I heard my mother call it the "crawl space," and I became intrigued with this enigma in the wall.

When I crawled inside, it was as if I had discovered a secret trap door leading to a mysterious place. I spent days cleaning the room, and seventeen full vacuum bags later the space was ready to furnish. I could barely stand up inside, and our doll furniture fit inside with perfect proportion. I found an old rug in the corner and laid it out along with all the pillows I could find. I brought all my special things inside—my first doll, my Matchbox cars, special rocks and shells. I brought a record player inside and put up a curtain at the entrance.

Shortly after I discovered this place it became apparent that it needed a name. "I am going to the crawl space" just didn't cut it. It became "The Hole" and was a place to play alone or with a friend. When we were inside it was as if we stopped existing in our parents' world. We were unaccountable. Whatever happened inside "The Hole" no one else would know. The place felt very safe, like a bomb shelter, and exciting, like another planet.

At age eleven there was a shift in the function of "The Hole" and the name changed to "The Whole." The focus of activity became primarily social. It was a place to hide friends who were running away or a place to listen to top 40 songs while a black light lit up music posters. It was a place to talk about who liked whom or to try smoking for the first time. As we got older, we frequented "The Whole" less and less and I hardly noticed the transition.[13]

Note the parallel here with the boys in Carriacou who stopped building bush houses and started building board houses around the age of twelve. "The Hole" served its protecting function, became transformed, and then was discarded when it was no longer needed, though as we will see it remained in Nancy's memory for future reference.

This final description was written by Catherine Sprague, age twenty-nine, who lived in rural Massachusetts when she was six years old.

When I was little and living in the Berkshires, the snow fell deep in the winters. I built myself a fort one winter by digging down straight into the snow and hollowing out a coffin-shaped ditch. There were other forts indoors and some secluded spots under hanging tree branches that I went to with friends. My snow fort is the one I remember best.

My fort seemed unique because no one I knew had ever built one like it. It was deep enough into the snow that, when I lay in it on my back, the steep walls blocked out most of the tops of the nearby trees and the roof of the house. It was deep enough that it insulated me from the cold.

I liked to go there because it was my special place. I imagined I couldn't be found. In my fantasies, the footprints leading to it and the snow I had piled up around the edges as I dug disappeared. Anyone would have to look very hard to find it. I felt alone and warm and safe. I was fascinated that the snow would keep me so warm. I thought of it as a room I had built for myself. Inside, I dug out little cubby holes in the sides for my mittens and stuff.[14]

These descriptions highlight the important qualities of the special-place experience as illustrated by adults' memories. Following are some specific components of the experience, as identified in these passages:

* Special places are found or constructed by children *on their own.* It is wonderful for parents to provide playhouses or build tree houses, but it is important for children to have the opportunity to build outside the parental field of vision.

* Special places are *secret.* Children do not want other people to know where they are, nor do they want to be found once they're inside. Not being seen is very important.

* Special places are *"owned"* by their creators. The flag raising and lowering ceremony in the first example is illustrative of the patriotism and commitment these children felt to their scrap of earth.

* Special places are *safe*. A feeling of calm and repose comes over children when they are in their special places. There is often a reflective or meditatively quiet aspect to being in these places. As Howard Thurman described, sitting against the oak allowed him to go inside himself and talk about his sorrows and joys. Bonnie says, *"Feeling the cool dirt beneath us sent a calming effect throughout our bodies."*

* Special places are *organized* worlds. Children love creating organized interior spaces suitable for storage of personal objects. Some children even create complex utility systems—simple plumbing and electricity really make your fort cool. Children like the process of building up a small world from scratch, of transforming natural or found materials into systems.

An additional aspect that characterizes almost all verbal recollections by adults of special places is a kind of breathless, twinkle-in-the-eye animation. It's thrilling for adults to revisit these places in their mind's eye, in part, I suspect, because they reexperience the explorer's feeling of claiming the world for their own, being the first on the scene, carving a civilized place out of the wilderness. It's like the process of selecting a campsite while backpacking in a trackless area. This place becomes home and security. Children are experiencing this in their own backyards, because they're exploring the world, on their own, for the first time.

THE RIGHT PLACE
AT THE RIGHT TIME

Certain developmental phenomena happen at very specific ages. The organism is keyed to certain biological unfoldings during specific time periods. Most children learn to walk somewhere between the tenth and fourteenth months. The loss of the first baby tooth around age six is used as an indicator of school readiness in Steiner schools. Language learning, as discussed earlier, unfolds along predictable developmental lines. The interest in, and perhaps need for, special, personal places seems to be one of those phenomena that occur during a closely prescribed time frame.

Louise Chawla criticizes Edith Cobb's notion that transcendent experiences in nature are peculiar to middle childhood. She found numerous accounts of similar experiences during adolescence. While I agree that there does not appear to be a developmental predisposition toward transcendent experience in middle childhood, my simple quantitative and more thorough qualitative findings suggest that fort building is most significant during the middle childhood years, particularly between ages eight and eleven. Prior to this age children are still fairly homebound, and after this age there is either a clear turning away from forts or a clear change in their function.

Roger Hart studied eighty-four children's free range, the distance from home children can travel without specific permission from parents.[15] He found a significant jump in the increase in range between second and third grade—right around the age of eight. There is a similar jump between fourth and fifth grade in the distances children travel from home. During this eight- to ten-year-old period, children are consistently pushing back the horizons of the known world. Robert Arbib, in *The Lord's Woods*, describes this early exploratory drive well:

I was nine years old that June afternoon so many years ago when we first discovered the Lord's Woods and the world was unspoiled and filled with mysteries. My first two-wheeler, dark red and fast, had come with my birthday in March, and ever since that glorious day my world had been expanding. Only yesterday I had ventured beyond the edge of my universe, out where

Westwood Road ceased to be paved and wound into the endless green unknown of the forest. . . .

We will know it all, Carl and I. We will explore and conquer this America of ours, we will make this our private paradise. To know it and, by knowing, own it, and then go forth beyond our woodland bounds, answering the urgent beckonings of field and farm and road and stream, the distant marsh horizon, . . . and the row of trees beyond the last ones we can see.[16]

As a boy, Arbib was drawn outward by what sounds almost like a magnetic force. In the process of these explorations, a safe home away from home was often necessary.

But then something happens. Between fifth and sixth grade, or between the ages of eleven and twelve, Hart found that children's average free range actually drops off. It is as if children become less interested in exploring, or getting away from home into the woods. Certainly some children persist in exploring, but as a group, there is a deeper biological tendency coming to the surface that changes children's behavior.

The following excerpts from adults' memories suggest why the shift away from forts and special places begins around this age. This first account is from Laurie Riley, eighteen, reflecting on a childhood experience in New Hampshire:

Jamestown was founded when I was in the third grade and

was my center of activity until halfway through the sixth grade. Jamestown was a private world located in a wooded area beyond a field that began at a stone wall. You had to step down from the stone wall into high grass. My brother Scott was our leader—like the chief of the village. Our individual houses were circular, built by piling sticks, and eventually we would place roofs using large, full pine boughs. There were roadways to each of our homes, a general meeting place, a trading post in the center of the village. Our activities were mainly preparing ourselves and our homes so that the bears could not get us. We also spent a great deal of time gathering objects for use in our individual homes. These activities at Jamestown seemed to fill our lives for a long time. We didn't exclude kids that we knew, but it seemed important that no adults be there, hear of, or even see our private world.

Somewhere in the middle of sixth grade, we were in Jamestown and someone started playing monster games. Everyone got carried away and each of our homes was destroyed. My house crumbled around me. Since that day, whenever I consider the age of Jamestown, I vividly remember that day and the ruins of my house. It seemed to clearly mark the beginnings of my wanting to hang around up in the girls' club that came into being. It was named the Venitians, after the planet Venus, because it was all girls who were stronger than any other humans.

My brothers, after a lapse of two years, returned to Jamestown and actually built a log cabin. The club that was formed was exclusive, particularly of girls. I never went to Jamestown after the day it was destroyed. I was into other things.[17]

During discussions of self-constructed rites of passage at puberty, I have discovered that many adults can recall similar experiences. One special form of these self-constructed rites for girls seems to be doll-play rituals that signify the end of childhood. Though I have uncovered only three accounts of this phenomenon, I suspect this is just the tip of an iceberg. Tina Staller, age thirty, described a memory from her sixth-grade year:

Margaret and I had a doll club, and one of the major activities of the club was having regular doll parties. All the dolls sat in chairs around small tables. A number of tea sets were used, and little cakes were served. Of course, each doll was groomed and dressed especially for the party. Or all the dolls would constitute a classroom of children and we would be teachers. Around the time we reached twelve, we started to feel self-conscious about our doll play. Doll play was for kids, and we were becoming young ladies. We decided to have one last gala event. All the dolls were decked out, a wonderful meal was prepared, and then, somewhat sadly, all of our dolls and all the trappings were put away for good. We never brought them out again.[18]

Marcia King, age thirty-seven and a sixth-grade teacher, read the previous description and was flooded with the memory of a similar ritual:

At the end of sixth grade, I felt the need to end the years of playing with dolls. After all, in a few months I would be going into junior high. I proceeded to collect all my dolls except for one, just in case. I packed that one up. I lined up all my other dolls, and cut their hair off. I sent several invitations off to friends inviting them to the funeral.

We walked down the road that day in a single-lined procession, pretending sadness, and walked through my beloved woods to the burial site [previously the site of her privately constructed playhouse]. *I found the special spot, and placed them carefully in the hole that I had dug up. I lead a made-up prayer and all my friends followed along. And, once again, I had let another part of my childhood go.*[19]

The image of the funeral is significant in Marcia's account. Rites of passage throughout the non-Western world are rife with the imagery of the death of childhood and the birth of adult responsibility. Lacking these social institutions, Western children often construct their own symbolic rites to signify the transformations they feel in themselves.

Jamestown, the Last Doll Party, and the Doll Funeral are illustrative of a significant developmental shift at puberty. At this point, many children tend to graduate from the private retreat in the woods or in the house to the social milieu of downtown. If, as suggested earlier, the special place is a cocoon within which the self is being formed, then around puberty the butterfly starts to emerge. The self is shaped enough to exist in the outside world.

In Devon, the oldest boys I worked with were only eleven years old. But when I asked Ben, the boy who did the most geographically accurate map of the local area, where his favorite place was, he said, *"At the W.H. Smith store in Newton Abbot* [a large market town about 4 miles from the hamlet of Denbury]. *There's neat computer games, books, maths and pens. I take the bus down there with my friends."* Ben did lots of exploring in the woods and had built a den recently by the River Dart, but his attention was starting to turn toward the world of commerce and social discourse.

Though I have conducted only a few mapping exercises with adolescents, they tend to focus on shops, schools, and their bedrooms more frequently than their younger counterparts. Biologically, their lives are changing, and their interests in special places changes from the solitary to the social.

THE VALUE OF REMEMBERING

After a presentation of my work with children to a group of parents and teachers at a small school in Devon, a lively conversation ensued. I was prepared for comments regarding curricular applications, children's safety, complaints that children don't do this anymore because all they ever do is watch television, and other serious adult concerns. Instead, I was regaled with stories about these adults' dens during their childhoods. One older woman remembered an experience from her childhood in London:

In between the houses were patches of garden that were allowed to grow wild. Tall grass grew up in here. We would mow a pathway down the center, then bend grass over from both sides and tie it in the middle with string to make a covered tunnel. Then we'd make rooms off of the main tunnel. It was my favorite place.

But then all the adults decided to tidy things up and mow these strips. A group of neighborhood children bonded together to ask parents not to cut select patches so we could use them for our dens, and they agreed. I think this is one of my earliest memories of a political activity.

Equally thought provoking was a comment from the director of this small school. She said,

When I'm tossing and turning and can't get to sleep at night, I rebuild the den up at the end of our road when I was ten. The smell of the fir trees while I put the boughs on the roof and relining the stones for the walkway and gate calm me down and put me to sleep.

Her comment made me realize that special places from childhood live on as "touchstone memories," memories that some adults return to time and again to savor in their mind's eye. As we all remember our first sexual experience, bitter or sweet, perhaps many of us remember the first times we made the world our own. Both experiences are similar in their qualities of discovery, of new realms opening up.

With my eyes opened to this possibility, I looked back through previously collected adult recollections to see if I could find other accounts of recurrent return to childhood places. I found some provocative examples of the persistence of these childhood special places into adulthood.

Carole Riley, age thirty-five, described her husband's and her own need to recapture some of the quality of their middle childhood play. They chose to *"build our new home on a hillside, in the woods, near a special rock, with a brook below us."* This place had been one of her husband's special places when he was nine to eleven years old. She further related the design of a sunken area in their living room to their desire to *"invite our children to turn this area into a ship, a fort, or a house within a house."* Their memories of these activities in childhood, and their specific attachment to the special rock, shaped their decision about where and how to build their adult home.[20]

Mary Morrisette, age forty, spoke poignantly about a childhood place and its loss during her adolescence. "Fairyland" on the shores of Lake Eden in Vermont was her retreat space for solitude until her parents sold it. *"What purpose is there of having special memories,"* she angrily demanded of her parents after the sale, *"if the place where the experiences happened isn't there anymore?"* Though hurt by the loss, Mary indicated that she now searches out places with a similar feeling wherever she lives in order to have access to that same kind of external and internal solitude. When she is faced with momentous decisions, she returns to her present day incarnation of Fairyland to *"sit, observe, and reflect."*[21]

Catherine Sprague, age twenty-nine, recalled her experiences of building her snow fort (described above) and the significance of the experience in her life:

I have thought about this fort over the last year, as I have been working through some dependencies in my adult life. My association with this place is one of it being the first independent action I can ever remember taking. The first time I went there, when I built it, my mother was angry with me because she couldn't find me. This was surprising to me; it was news that I could do something all by myself, for myself, that would affect someone else. Her anger didn't diminish my good feelings about the place. I think, in a way, it deepened them, made the place more mine. There was a feeling of success.[22]

Nancy Segreto, age twenty-eight, creator of "The Hole," confirms this sense of empowerment:

The crawl space was my first "apartment" away from home. Each time I move to a new place that appears run down and dirty, I imagine how nice I could make it, how special its features are. I associate feelings of strength, independence, and free will with my transformation of "The Hole." It was nothing before I discovered it. Since I did it then, I can do it again.[23]

Whether it's the political activity of bonding together to save a patch of grass for fort building or the personal activity of a first independent action, making a place in the world starts the individual on the pathway toward self-definition, toward action in the world and the birth of the self.

A SEPARATE HEARTH

Excerpts from a reflective essay by Kim Stafford, an American nature writer, summarize the significance of special places. Coming upon this essay was like discovering that I had a twin who was separated from me at birth. Here was the quintessential literary expression of the ideas I was pursuing from a psychological perspective. I was stunned. I recommend "The Separate Hearth" from *Having Everything Right* to anyone compelled by these ideas.[24]

Between the ages of eight and fifteen, the author spent most of his out-of-school time exploring The Woods, a two-mile-by-three-mile swath of woods on the edge of urban Portland, Oregon. Feeling alternately like Lewis and Clark and Robinson Crusoe, he and his friends explored the expanse of this world, foraged and hunted, and created private worlds.

When I went to The Woods alone, my experience was shaped by a book [my grandmother] had given me, Theodora Kroeber's Ishi in Two Worlds. *Like Ishi, I was the last man, the only man of a lost tribe. I too had a small, sacred geography hidden even from my friends. . . . A huge tree had fallen, and where the root-mass tore out from the earth a hollow was left that no one could see, roofed over with the arched limbs of fir, woven with sword fern and moss, with leaf litter, until the roof became a knob of the earth itself. Like Ishi, I approached by a different way each time, so as not to wear a path, and I covered the entrance to my den with boughs broken, not cut in a human way.*

Axiom 1: During the middle childhood years, children feel a deep urge to move into the larger world away from home to find a place for themselves. Secrecy creates a sense of satisfying isolation.

In the woods by myself, fire was the heart of it all. In my secret den, or in some refuge off the trail, I would seek out the low shade-killed twigs of a hemlock tree, and the ritual of isolation and sufficiency would begin. I would hold a broken branch to my lips to see how dry it was. I would lay a ring of stones dug into mineral soil and arrange perfect sticks one over the other. I would slip out one match from the gleaming steel safe in my pocket, peel off the paraffin cap from its head with my thumbnail, and shield the hearth with my body from the wind— **this was the repeated prelude to my identity.** *When the match burst open in my cupped hands, and the flame climbed obediently through the precise architecture of my kindling, I had made again,* **my own portable world in the world.** [Author's emphasis.]

Axiom 2: The fort, or the special place, is a concrete manifestation of the abstract sense of self that is born in adolescence. The person makes a literal place in the world in childhood preparatory to making a figurative place in the world in adolescence and adulthood.

Here was my private version of civilization, my separate hearth. Back home, there were other versions of this. I would take any refuge from the thoroughfare of plain living—the doll-house, the tree-house, furniture, the tablecloth tent, the attic, the bower in the cedar tree. I would take any platform or den that got me above, under, or around the corner from the everyday. There I pledged allegiance to what I knew, as opposed to what was common. My parents' house was a privacy from the street, from the nation, from the rain. But I did not make that house, or find it, or earn it with my own money. It was given to me. My separate hearth had to be invented by me, kindled, sustained, and held secret by my own soul as a rehearsal for departure.

Axiom 3: Through making special places, children are experiencing themselves as shapers and makers of small worlds. This experience contributes to making them active shapers of the world in their adult lives.

Is this a necessity for education—that each child must have some kind of separate hearth, some separate fire to kindle in secret?

Axiom 4: Educators should acknowledge the unique world-making desires of middle childhood and shape curriculum to provide appropriate experiences in and out of schools.

Stafford's emphasis on the hearth and the fire within the special place adds a new dimension to the discussion. If the fort or den is symbolically the self, perhaps the fire is the soul, the life force that lives within the individual. The fire makes the house a home, gives the individual a living center. Are we kindling this fire in children we teach or dousing the flames with premature abstraction?

If children's fort-making and world-shaping inclinations discussed here are universal, then rich educational opportunities are indicated. One of the strongest memories I have of fifth grade is the book report I did on *Born Free*, the story of Elsa the lion. As a variation from the norm for book reports, my teacher provided the option of creating a diorama of a scene from the book. I tilted a PF Flyers sneakers box on its side and created a little bit of Africa. I still remember the cottony clouds, bushes secured in modeling plastic, the waterhole, the details of this small world within a box. It was one of the few opportunities we had in elementary school to shape a small world. Clearly, more are needed.

5

MAKING A PLACE
IN THE CURRICULUM

Alex led the way down the bank and into a dark tunnel through the brambles. *"Cat's Alley,"* he murmured back at me. *"We call it that because in the summer, only cats can make it through here."* On my hands and knees, I scrambled along the passageway and found Alex sitting with his legs crossed next to an abandoned fifty-five-gallon drum. *"My secret den,"* he whispered. *"No one knows about this place, even my brother."* We were huddled in a little dome-shaped clearing that he had carved out of the thicket. As I sat there, I felt simultaneously honored and intrusive. I felt privileged to be able to share in his secret but questioned my right to be there. Did my presence take away from the value of this place for Alex? Should adults poke their noses into children's secret places?

It is important to begin this consideration of curriculum with a disclaimer. Some aspects of children's experiences are better left alone. Although it is a completely valid objective of progressive educators to relate the curriculum to the child's life, I have a sense that there are realms in which the adult should not trespass. If secrecy is an important element of the special place, then it is important not to pressure children into unfolding their secrets. Often during my research with children I felt as if I was about to cross the line. Certainly I made a point of telling children that I was interested in having them show me their places, but it was completely up to them to decide if they wanted to take me. Some children deferred, but most were enthusiastic. After all, sometimes a secret isn't any good unless you can share it.

For the most part, however, educators could be doing much more to offer curricular opportunities in place making. What follows is a variety of case studies of children and teachers at work. I have attempted to choose examples from urban and rural settings and with younger and older children to demonstrate the many ways in which the place-making tendencies of middle childhood can be utilized in the schools.

THE EXPLORERS' CLUB

The Harrisville School, Harrisville, NH
Amy Carter, Teacher
Children: Aged five to seven

On Wednesday afternoons, the kindergartners and first graders at The Harrisville School become explorers. Like mail carriers in any kind of weather (well, not in downpours), Amy Carter takes her bands of adventurers out for forays around the village and woods of this lakeside New Hampshire village. (See figure 5-1.)

I realized that if I wanted to do exploring of the local environment on a regular basis, I needed a forum, so we created The Explorers' Club. Then, in an early brainstorming session about what explorers do, one of the children said, "If we're going to be a club, then we need a clubhouse." The rest of the children immediately became excited. "Or a tree fort!" others suggested excitedly. We were off and running.

Amy and her assistant teacher, Jane, divided the class into two groups of eight children each and searched the woods for appropriate sites—not too close to school, not too far, special in some way. Amy's group chose a site next to a large granite boulder with a few fallen trees nearby.

117

EXPLORERS

On Wednesday afternoons the Explorers' Club spent a lot of time exploring the forest behind school. We learned how to use compasses, built forts and nature trails, and climbed huge rocks. We observed the seasonal changes and looked closely at many tiny things.

SPECIAL SPOT

FORT

BARN

SCHOOL

WHILE EXPLORING IN THE WOODS WE....

found caterpillars.
saw lots of bugs on leaves.
built a fort with a bouncy-board trail.
saw Mayflowers all over the place.
went way out in the deep woods and caught
    dragonflies with our bare hands.
built fairyhouses and collected food and furniture
    for them.

IN THE POND WE.....

caught frogs and frog eggs.
went into the water and almost fell in.
caught monster bugs, worm houses, water boatmen,
water striders, tadpoles, and a giant stinkbug.
held a snake.
found worm houses made out of sticks + grass.
watched the monster bug kill a tadpole.

FIGURE 5-1 From the Harrisville School Yearbook 1987–1988— a collection of children's work with teacher's narrative. Maps and pictures by children.

With much architectural assistance from Amy, the children built a clubhouse during the next three Wednesday afternoons. Branches were leaned up against the boulder and then covered with leaves. A pathway leading to the fort was lined with fallen birch logs and a bridge was made over a wet spot. Decisions for furnishing the interior were made as a group—ferns for carpets, moss for a secret garden in the corner, glowworms for lights, pine needle pillows.

The Explorers' Clubhouse served as the base from which to explore. One of the first activities the teachers developed was to have children find a special spot, their own place. The spots had to be within talking distance of the clubhouse, far enough way to be private but not too far or it would be too scary. These spaces were more found than constructed, but small modifications were made. Children would go as a group to the clubhouse and then spend twenty to thirty minutes at their special spots. They'd spend time alone or visit. Children were then asked to choose three things that made their spot unique and write about or draw them.

The Explorers' Club moved indoors on some of the cold, wet, dreary winter days. Amy and Jane suggested building forts indoors and the children were enthralled.

Fort building inside was okay at home, but in school? This activity lasted for parts of three days and was extended to included miniforts, constructions made out of clay, straw, and toothpicks.

In the spring, children found that their clubhouses had lasted the winter, fairly intact, and the sites again became the focal point for further explorations: climbing the big rock, getting lost, throwing rocks in the marsh.

Jane commented on the club at the end of the school year:

Of all the wonderful things that happened this year, the special spots activity was most remarkable. We would just go up into the woods, the children would go off to their special spots, and things would start to happen. They seemed so placid and calm and self-directed when we were there. It just seemed so right for them.

This description of Amy's explorers/forts curriculum fascinated me because the form was a perfect translation of my research into action. Particularly intriguing was the two-stage process of creating a group fort and then having individuals find their own special places. This was how the children of Buttercombe Close arranged their den—a hollowed out hedge with a separate room for each child. It is appropriate for children aged five to seven to create places together and then have a small space within or closely associated. The desire for an isolated, faraway place becomes much more important between the ages of nine and eleven.

The progression from outside forts to inside forts to miniaturized forts is also of curricular value. Having created a full-sized clubhouse, the children understood the notion of shrinking it to a model. This process could be a good introduction to other small-worlds activities. Variation in scale is an accessible idea for children this age if activities include concrete experiences and materials.

MY SIDE OF THE MOUNTAIN

Guilford Central School, Guilford, VT
Amos Fortune, Teacher
Children: Aged nine and ten

Harris Center for Conservation Education,
Hancock, NH
Jan Altobell, Teacher
Children: Aged ten and eleven

My Side of the Mountain by Jean Craighead George is a wonderful literary expression of making a home for yourself in the woods. Fourth- and fifth-grade teachers in the same school often argue over who should get to read this to the class. In my mind, there are few books that resonate so deeply for children at this developmental stage.

Sam Gribley, a twelve-year-old, creates his own rite of passage by running away to his grandfather's land in the Catskills, north of New York City, and living in the wild. He makes a home for himself by burning and carving out the center of an old massive hemlock tree and turning it into a cozy, warm livable space. He spends the winter here and hunts and forages for most of his own food. Children's eyes glaze over in fascination when they hear this transformation of the tree described. *"If only I could do that,"* they muse to themselves.

Rider Foley, a fourth grader in Guilford, got the encouragement he needed. Amos Fortune suggested as a book report option that children build a fort like the one in the story, take pictures of it, and write a description of how they built it. I visited Rider's lean-to, built with his sister, in November 1988.

We only used a hatchet and jackknife to build it. No other tools. First we leaned branches up against this big tree, then crisscrossed these with little twigs, then put on leaves and dirt. When it rains, you can stay completely dry inside. In winter, we could walk right up to the top because it was so strong. It's not like you could walk up a regular pile of sticks—they'd crunch. Mr. Fortune says when you make it dome shaped, then the weight is distributed around. This lean-to is better than the fort that my father helped us build because we made this without any nails and it's more in the woods. It also keeps us warmer in the winter.

When I asked Rider if it was his favorite place, he said that last year it was his favorite place, but this year he liked the hollow maple way off in the woods. Whereas this lean-to was about one hundred meters from the house, the mammoth hollow maple, complete with its own draw-bridge, was a half mile away. Rider could actually climb down inside this tree, and as soon as he could go there by himself, he had plans to improve it.

Rider's written report was complete with pictures, description, and evident pride. It's worth noting that without the literary impetus and the teacher's suggestion, this lean-to probably would not have been built. By giving fort building validity and a place in the curriculum, Rider's teacher nudged him from interest into actualization.

Jan Altobell, environmental educator for the Harris Center for Conservation Education in the Hancock, New Hampshire, public schools decided to do a full-day field trip to give students a true back-to-the-woods experience. Her description suggests the value of this kind of genuine field trip, a field trip predicated on a deep understanding of developmental inclinations. Keep in mind that this description and the children's comments were given without any cognizance of my research and writing.

My Side of the Mountain Day had finally arrived. The children had been reading Jean George's classic book for weeks and had been imagining Sam Gribley's life in the wilderness. They had been learning about and tasting edible wild plants, like birch twigs, cattail tubers, and wintergreen leaves. On this particular day, small groups of fifth graders would be led into the woods by enthusiastic parents to build homes, forage, and make something useful using fifteen feet of twine. They also would spend some time alone writing about their experiences.

Unlike twelve-year-old Sam Gribley, . . . some kids made elaborate shelters around fallen, rotting trees that suggested a protective outline of a home. Others built roofs that connected one huge boulder to another. Each house design was inspired by the site and the available materials, and each one was distinctly different from the others.

Some of the most interesting things to see were all the objects that the kids had crafted using twine—an apple dryer, a broom, hammers, a table, a spear, a bench, a toilet, a shelf, a clothesline, a trap. One group made acorn-top whistles and created a code for blowing signals to their shelter mates. Three short toots meant "Return to the kitchen!" One long toot meant "Help!"

Basking under the apple trees in the warm October sun, we reflected on the day and recorded our thoughts in our journals.

Here are some samples:

"I like depending on myself in the woods. The roof caved in on me, so we built another one more slowly. It was stronger. I imagine it will be up a long time."

"I wouldn't do what Sam Gribley did. I would miss my parents and bed with stuffed animals."

"I would like a home in the woods that I could go to whenever I feel like it. I would stay there for a weekend or a month, but not in cold weather. It would be hard to find food. I would bring some with me."

"I like Hidden Haven. It is good and stable. It has a slide and table and bathroom. There is a place for a fire and EVERYTHING ELSE."

*"I like having woods so I have a place where nobody bothers me. It is private. I can pretend and make up stories. **The woods are my home and our house is my parents' house."*** [Author's emphasis.]

On the bus ride back to Keene most of us snoozed, our faces glowing from the sun and wind. I felt a tap on my shoulder and turned around to see Flannery pointing out the window toward Old Concord Road, north of town. "Mrs. Altobell, I'm going to build a fort right back there when I get home." I smiled and contemplated the power and challenge of my mission as a nurturer of children's compassion for nature.[1]

Jan Altobell provides us with an example of what I have come to refer to as authentic curriculum. By authentic curriculum I mean curriculum that emerges out of the long-standing collective unconscious of the students themselves as opposed to curriculum that is imposed on or poured into children. In this case, Jan Altobell recognized the longing for place making that is ascendant in children this age and created curriculum to provide for the exploration and expression of these desires. The validation of place making as legitimate encouraged both Rider and Flannery to go out and do it themselves. This is education at its best, where academic content and deep personal and developmental interests flow together like two streams merging into one.

URBAN FORTS

East Harlem District Four School and
Central Park Conservancy
Sally Austin, Teacher
Children: Aged eleven and twelve

Forts in Harlem? Well maybe in abandoned buildings or under the fire escape or in refrigerator boxes in the basement, but tree forts? Yes. Sally Austin, director of the North

End Discovery Program in Central Park, discovered the way to do it.

Here are all these kids in East Harlem, cooped up in apartment buildings, and most of them never get into the park. Our objective was to familiarize children with the park so that they could start to consider it part of their community. With two sixth-grade classes, we conducted treasure hunts, made topographical maps of the North End, and talked to the planners, tree climbers, and rangers in the park. It worked great, but there was still something missing. I wanted kids to be able to make places of their own as a way of feeling at home in the park, but that seemed impossible. When we weren't worried about flashers or drug pushers in the isolated sections of the park, we'd be finding discarded hypodermic needles or prophylactics. It's hard to feel safe in those circumstances.

But then we stumbled upon it. The landscape crews cart all the leaves, broken tree limbs, and excavated dirt to a storage area adjacent to the North Meadow. Here, leaves are gradually composted and trees cut up into firewood, but in the meantime, there's a wealth of fort-building materials, and nobody really cares if you mess things up. It's become one of the favorite places for children to return to, and their forts are now showing up on their maps.

Urban parks can serve the valuable function of giving

children "loose parts" to use in the construction of their own places. Teachers often pass over these places as field trip sites in favor of the zoo, the aquarium, or museums, places they perceive as more intellectually stimulating. In fact, children might benefit more from activities encouraging them to create places, something they may not do on their own. In this way, they may become supporters and protectors of these urban green spaces.

THE ARLINGTON HUTS

Preshil School, Melbourne, Australia
Kimberly Dovey, Researcher
Children: Aged five through twelve

Kimberly Dovey's documentation of forty years of hut building on the campus of a private, progressive school in Melbourne provides a description of the different stages of building and the school's policies regarding this form of children's play.

From the earliest days, hut building was an integral part of everyday life. It was considered a natural extension of formal educational activity and of the task-based education philosophy of the school. It was, however, not a programmed activity but a spontaneous one, not something that was very organized but rather something that was not stopped.

Huts ranged from sticks arranged on the ground by the youngest children to constructed, enclosed huts by the seven- and eight-year-olds to elevated, multilevel tree forts by the "biggies." However, in the early 1980s, all hut building was formally ended. Neighbors were complaining about the un- sightly huts and the fire department ordered the "treehouses dismantled and removed" and "frequent and prompt removal of all accumulated waste and unnecessary combustible materials."

A few years later, hut building was revived in a for- mal manner.

The huts began with a class project, limited to the oldest children, whereby they were to simulate a preindustrial commu- nity, building huts in groups using preindustrial materials and techniques. It was quite common for class projects to involve the transformation of various parts of the school grounds. Rules were set by teachers—all huts were to be on the ground, and they must not be visible from the street. The regulations excluded boards and packing crates and led to the use of branches and leaves for good camouflage. . . . Some of the huts were half underground with seats hollowed out of the earth.

About these new huts, one child commented:

No one's allowed to build any more huts unless they're for special things. It was work; we were learning things from it. I mean we'd learned things from building our own huts as well, but they [the neighbors and the fire department] didn't think of it that way.

Kim Dovey summarizes his account:

What lessons might the case of the Arlington huts hold for our understanding of children's environments? I think it stands as an example of the manner in which the childhood imperative for place making can be integrated into the schoolground as a spontaneous and meaningful cultural practice. In a context where urban wildlands are being eradicated and children's access to the landscape is increasingly diminished by cars and crime, the possibilities for place-making activities as a part of school life become more important.[2]

Place making on the school grounds can take a variety of forms. I have seen

* the creation of a simulated Abnaki village in woods adjacent to the playground;

* the construction of a six-foot-by-eight-foot authentic log cabin built in a parking lot adjacent to the school, which was then reassembled on the teacher's land as a garden shed.

* the creation of an ecosphere, a kind of life-sized terrarium, complete with a turtle pond and living shrubs and meadow, created inside the classroom. This

eight-square-foot enclosure became a research site for middle school ecology studies.

* the building of a bird blind in a nature study area adjacent to a school.

All these formal constructions serve a purpose different from child-created spaces but are useful examples of how children respond to place-making activities.

SCHOOLYARD VILLAGES

Roxaboxen, by Alice McLerran,
illustrated by Barbara Cooney
A children's book describing a children's village.

The Forts at Jonathan Daniels Elementary School,
Keene, New Hampshire

The Children's Village at the Waldorf School
of Cape Cod, Falmouth, Massachusetts
described by Sally Stevens.

The forts at the George Soule School,
South Freeport, Maine
described by Patrice O'Neill Maynard.

Alice McLerran's recently published *Roxaboxen* is a portrait of a children's village in the southwestern United

States. Created spontaneously by about a dozen neighborhood children in the 1930s, the village was constructed of discarded boxes, scrap wood, and stones. Each child created his or her own home, outlined in stones. Then streets emerged, as well as bakeries, ice cream shops, and the mayor's office. Seen by adult eyes, this place would have looked like casually organized flotsam and jetsam on a faceless ridge in the desert. But to the children who created it, it was a vibrant minisociety.

This book is just one example I have found of children's villages—small societies constructed by and for children with no adult intervention. Certainly Jamestown, described in chapter four, is an example of one of these. The Arlington Huts come close. But what makes these places not just a congregation of structures but actual villages is the social dynamic that emerges when these places have longevity. To make a world in which to find a place to discover a self, there must be a social fabric so that diversified rules and roles can be developed.

In the fall of 1990, I observed "The Forts" on the playground at the Jonathan Daniels Elementary School in Keene, New Hampshire. (See figure 5-2.) These forts illustrated the seminal stage of an emergent village. In this case, the third graders described the forts as an outgrowth of talk of "war" between the boys and the girls. Many of

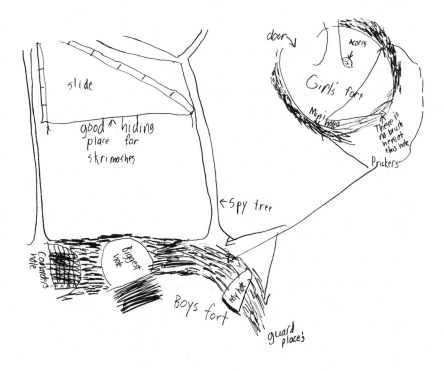

FIGURE 5-2 Diagram drawn by third-grade student showing boys'
and girls' forts on playground at Jonathan Daniels School in Keene,
New Hampshire, in fall 1990.

133

the lower branches of the trees adjacent to the playground had recently been pruned, so the children had a good source of "loose parts" to fuel their construction desires. Peter, a third grader, described the forts:

The boys and girls were getting edgy because of talk of war, so we went out to build forts. I mean, who wants to hide behind a tree? The teachers said we couldn't go into the woods, so we did with what we had and collected the cut down branches. The boys built a long barricade, and the girls build a fort in the shape of a big U, like a nest. There were a few skirmishes. During the edgy times, we used prickers as barbed wire. We'd look through loopholes and take up acorns and fire them through the holes. Our commander would shinny up the spy tree to see what the girls were doing.

Kate, another third grader, continued,

The boys wouldn't let us in their fort, so sometimes we ran through to see where their spying holes were, and we'd try to steal sticks so we could make our fort bigger. But now we're getting together and I don't think we'll get so upset. The girls are joining the boys' garrison, and we're putting our forts together. The one fort will be strong and secure—it's like a luxury fort because who would want to go against us now? With no more edgy stuff, it's more fun to be in the forts.[3]

During these early stages, issues over property ownership, boundaries, rules of interaction are an issue for children. But as the structures within a space evolve and increase in number; social order starts to develop.

The Children's Village at the Waldorf School of Cape Cod began in the fall of 1988 when the school moved to a new building. There was no playground and no money to build one, so the children had to create one out of nothing. By the end of the first year, there was a village of tepeelike structures in place. Since then the village has continued to evolve. From time to time there is a store that uses shells and leaves for currency. At one point there was a bank that issued paper money and kept records. But the bank got robbed and the banker decided it was too much trouble to keep track of the paper money. A culture is emerging.

Culture has flourished at the Soule School in South Freeport, Maine. Similar to the Arlington Huts, "The Forts" have been around since the school was built about twenty-five years ago. The Forts area comprises about three-fourths of an acre of wooded space that has little under-brush adjacent to the school playground. Over the years, an autonomous children's culture has been allowed to evolve, almost completely independent of adult or teacher intervention. The Forts are a children's world, and children are encouraged to work out problems independently. When The Forts were studied by Patrice Maynard during the spring of 1990, she described the way in which they were used:

Teachers would become a bit annoyed when asked to mediate arguments about The Forts. It was made clear that The Forts were kid things, and arguments should be kept and settled there. Teachers made it clear that they would intervene only if they absolutely had to, and then if they did have to, they made it clear through their demeanor that it was not what they wanted to be doing.[3]

On occasion, the teachers provided indoor discussion time for working out issues.

In spring 1990, about forty second through fifth graders were actively involved in sustaining six to seven forts. Some forts were elaborate. The fifth graders' fort included a castle, a bank, a gate of entry, and the largest area. All forts were segregated by sex, and most were organized by grade-level groupings. Of striking interest was the monetary system that had emerged based on chunks of blacktop that had been broken up. This blacktop, with high mica content, glittered more than average blacktop. With surprising consistency, children agreed about the relative worth of different sized chunks. Maynard describes the system:

A four-inch-wide chunk of the stuff universally elicited a $20 valuation from a dozen children. This money can be traded for different commodities. Corn, for instance, is a necessity. Corn is a food, and if one's fort has no corn, it is without food. Corn is *actually dried cinnamon fern, and a bunch of corn about an inch in diameter at the stems costs $20.*[4]

This consistency is a testimony to the elaboration of traditions that have stabilized over the years. Maynard was also able to elicit the code of ethics, the rules that children had developed. These were offered up by a small group of children and then verified in interviews with other children.

1. No war Forts. No sticks or guns as weapons.
2. If you quit, you can't rejoin unless everybody in the Fort agrees.
3. Everybody has to vote you in. If one person doesn't want you, you can't get in [though each Fort has its own ways of letting people in— some don't ever vote].
4. No stealing from other people's Forts.
5. If you're gone from your Fort for two weeks, somebody else can take your Fort. [This point is debatable.]
6. Nobody can kick you out of a Fort once you are in.
7. You can't go in other people's Forts unless you're invited or you're selling things.

Maynard also reflected on the significance of The Forts in the children's lives:

The depth of the personal feelings woven into the rules and unspoken proprieties of Fort activities is impressive. It is this that leads to the speculation that the very existence of The Forts allows for a level of consciousness about the environment, about the earth, not possible without them. Violations of The Fort area are equivalent to personal violations. One weekend, there were marauders who vandalized the whole Fort area and took some things out of The Forts and uncovered secret places. It took several days of small meetings that were like therapy sessions to settle everyone's feelings about the incident. The children took it very personally. It would seem that this is an important feeling to foster on an earth that needs protecting.

It is interesting to wonder about the relationship between The Forts and the development of the children's environmental action group named CAKE (Concern about Kids' Environment) that was born at this school. Concerned about the amount of Styrofoam from the local McDonald's, a school group conducted a successful campaign that led to the passing of an ordinance by the town to ban Styrofoam. The campaign received national coverage on the "Today Show" and in World magazine. Recently, one of the CAKE kids was chosen by the organization "Giraffe" [for people who stick their necks out for the earth] *to go on a trip to the USSR to describe their work for the environment.*

Since then, CAKE chapters have been spawned at schools throughout New England. Since The Forts predate the CAKE activities by twenty-five years, it is worth speculating about how much the connection with the earth through The Forts helped to bring the children to the awareness that enabled the Styrofoam protest to take place.[5]

Maynard's final point is compelling. Environmental education curricula often prematurely invite elementary teachers and students to get involved in global issues. Saving dolphins and rain forests and endangered species is fine, but do children really have any sense of what this means? Authentic environmental commitment emerges out of firsthand experiences with real places on a small, manageable scale. The depth of involvement of these students with The Forts, with independence and autonomy ensured by the teachers, perhaps created the matrix, the fertile soil, in which true values of ownership and commitment could grow. Feeling like they owned The Forts, the children gained a sense of authority and, I hesitate to use the word, empowerment. It was then an appropriate, accessible step to taking on a local, visible issue like Styrofoam. The next question then is: Can we create curriculum that makes the connection between place making and social action? The Game of Village is the best example that I know of.

THE GAME OF VILLAGE

Summer Programs in Nelson, New Hampshire
Cia Iselin, Founder
Children: Aged ten through fourteen

Kimball Elementary School, Concord, New Hampshire
Kathleen Mitchell, Teacher
Children: Aged eleven through twelve

The Game of Village is an insightful translation of children's interest in constructing spaces into developmentally appropriate curriculum. Village started as a summer camp program for middle school children in rural New Hampshire. Simply stated, the idea was for a group of children to spend the summer creating a community in miniature. From this simple idea has grown a year-long project rooted in children's deep interests and elaborating into sophisticated and complex social studies, environmental science, language arts, and mathematics curricula.

Village sprang from two main sources of inspiration. One source was founder Cia Iselin's recognition of the value of children's play:

My children used to call it "playing in little." I know of no more elegant description. Playing in little goes beyond playing with toys or building perfect scale models. It implies seeing in little and being in little as well. To get into this world it is necessary to undergo a transformation. This faculty is available only to persons who have maintained their lively imagination and can slip in and out of the scene beneath them, becoming a miniature person for a "wrinkle in time." Instead of scorning "child's play," . . . it is time to put it to work.

Living and dreaming in miniature was a lifelong habit my husband and I shared. We had a lovely ambition about building a gigantic miniature installation that would allow people to see the world, much in the way that astronauts have since seen it, from above. This would enable decision makers to see whole forests before they started managing trees.[6]

This lifelong dream was given specific form when the Iselins traveled to Holland and came upon Madurodam, a miniature Dutch village constructed on four acres built on the scale of 1:25. Here are 130 faithful tiny reproductions of Dutch originals, from scenes of farms surrounded by canals to the elegant parliament buildings and even the modern Schiphol International Airport. Trains run on schedule, lights come on automatically in the evenings, a miniature world lives and breathes before your eyes.

141

Ms. Iselin describes how visiting this village inspired her to create the educational program of Village:

When our incessant search for miniature models finally brought us to the gates of Madurodam, we were ecstatic. Here was the incarnation of our dreams. We stayed a week and persuaded the management to let us have a look behind the scenes. . . . One morning an engineer from the Nederlands Railroad, responsible for the operation of the Madurodam line, showed us around the control room. Our guide was interrupted by the appearance of a young woman who was the landscape architect for the little town. She had come to discuss plans for the placement of some new flowering bulbs. The discussion was polite but became heated when she discovered that the Nederlands Railroad had other plans for the site she had chosen. Our eyes met in a flash that said, "If grown ups can take this game so seriously, what would children do with it?" In that moment, the game of Village was conceived.[7]

What children have done with it, and how teachers have used it, is testimony to the possibilities inherent in curriculum based on honoring children's inherent drive to shape and create the world. The following description of Village in a classroom setting was presented to the Concord, New Hampshire, school board by sixth-grade teacher Kathleen Mitchell.

The Structure of Village

Creating a Peep: The Village project is a simulation game in which youngsters create a miniature village or community and, in doing so, explore the connections between nature and people. Each child creates a character, a small person, called a "peep," to represent him- or herself in this community that is to be developed. Each child begins with the same materials, but each peep is unique. The pipe cleaners, yarn, and wooden balls are transformed into bones and muscles of varying size, tying in with the students' study of the human body. Then everyone takes needle and thread to clothe the peeps, since nudism is discouraged in the Village. Language arts activities are highlighted as individual peeps need a personality, an identity, and a history. We have group meetings where peeps introduce themselves to the entire group of potential homesteaders.

Land Exploration and Homestead Agreements: As land commissioner, the teacher presents the idea of homesteading, and the students review what they know about American pioneers and homesteaders. We research additional details to answer the specific questions that arise. Then come visits to White Farm (a local environmental education site owned by the school district) to look for appropriate sites to settle. The class breaks up into teams to find the perfect site and then tries to "sell" the rest of the class on their choice. This is the beginning of the town meeting concept. After a quick review of parliamentary procedure, the students run the meeting. Once a group decision is reached (and this is not ever easy), the class uses compasses and tape measures to carefully mark and map their mini-acre of land. The next step is to review the proprietary rights agreement that they will take to the assistant superintendent for a signature. The superintendent always questions the group about the contractual details of proprietary rights, eminent domain, public domain, and land title responsibilities.

Back at White Farm, the homesteaders study natural resources and land use as they prepare for homesteading. Math activities dealing with area and perimeter suddenly become more meaningful as peeps are concerned with getting the most area for their 864 minifeet of perimeter. Measurement activities using minirulers, on a scale of 1:24, and ratio and proportion are next.

Town Government: The group studies different forms of government so they can select the type that they feel will be best. We have had a selectmen form of government for Littleton Village and a city council form for Peepsburg, in spite of my lobbying for a benevolent monarchy. Ironically, many of the peeps feel that their jobs and homes demand so much time that they really can't afford the time or aggravation involved in public service. However, full-fledged elections take place, and somehow dedicated public servants do take charge.

Developing Properties: The next great event is Homesteading Day. All peeps who have registered for the project by introducing themselves participate in a land rush. Despite my concerns about the loss of life and limb, this part of the process works. Everyone manages to safely find a plot of land, to mark it, to fence it, and to make a detailed map for the land commissioner. Fencing is tougher than it sounds, because peeps have no money to buy fences, and they have to use available materials to create a secure boundary. The peeps return to school, where they meet with the land commissioner to sign Homestead Agreements, which detail the rights and responsibilities of each homesteader. Contract law is an integral part of Village, and the land commissioner is no pushover.

Building a House: First, each peep needs to have a primitive shelter in which he/she resides until the permanent home is completed. These are constructed of raw materials found on the site. The requirement is that they must be weatherproof so that peeps can actually stay there overnight and in between students' visits to the site

145

without being damaged. The students then begin design work on their permanent structures. These are sketched first and then done to scale. Once these are complete, the peeps begin work on foundations and landscaping. The more you do to your property, the more it will be worth. It's at this point that waste disposal, trespassing, public roads, and riparian rights become issues that need to be discussed by the community. Town meetings occur regularly and are run entirely by the peeps.

Village Bank and Trading Post: Over the next few days, the peeps open a bank, alias an Apple computer with an Appleworks spreadsheet. Each peep receives the enormous sum of 500 minidollars (interest free) in return for homesteading, but the peep can borrow at 10 percent interest on the value of his/her land. All expenses are listed for each account by the "highly paid" bankers, but each peep has to keep track of money in an individual checkbook as well.

Peeps go to the trading post to buy building materials. Some extravagant ideas about building are tempered by the reality of material costs. The 500 minidollars quickly disappear, as each sheet of cardboard costs 200 minidollars and masking tape runs 10 minidollars per minifoot. This is before we even deal with paint, carpeting, fancy fences, wallpaper, or furniture; they're all extra. I received a call from a mother who wondered why her daughter had come home complaining about the high costs of housing, the low pay of public employees, and the problems of trying to make a decent life for your family.

Vocations and Professions: Students obtain jobs working for the community or creating products that are needed by the community. Some peeps become furniture makers, others become doctors who can surgically repair peep limbs (for a price of course). One enterprising group of students staked claim to a heap of clean sand and created the Ready Mix Concrete enterprise. Another group created a zoo, complete with peepagators, for those spare recreational moments not tied up by building your house or going to meetings. A monetary system develops; a newspaper is created. Last year we even had a Peepingdales department store. The youngsters quickly realize that recreational facilities are popular and profitable, just as the state of New Hampshire has.

The Minifair: At the end of the project, we hold the ever-popular minifair for other students, relatives, and friends. Family members are often dragged out to the Village on weekends or after school. Everything is still in miniature form. Visitors can purchase naked pseudopeeps for the event, and they can buy accessories as well as minipizzas, minicookies, and minilemonade to refresh themselves after the riverboat and balloon rides. Visitors clothe their peeps and then take them on the rides created for their miniature people. It's a well-attended event with unsuspecting parents in shiny shoes and business clothes who stagger through high brush and deep mud to see what their kids have been talking about all these weeks.

Appraisals and the Mini-Auction: The fair is followed by an appraisal of all properties by the land commissioner and town officials. Data are transferred to the computer and peeps pay back their loans. After their finances are in order, there is a mini-auction. Peeps can bid on mini-items purchased at French's Toy Store with the proceeds of the fair. The amount of money a peep has to spend is the difference between the appraised value of the peep's property and how much money has to be paid to the bank for expenses.

Why Village Works in the Curriculum: I have conducted Village with two completely different classes. One was the most difficult group I have ever worked with. Their primary interests were sex and rock 'n' roll, in that order. Yet they responded enthusiastically to Village. Even to this day, over half those youngsters have come back to reminisce about the activity. Many still have their peeps— somewhat unusual for jaded eighth graders. The second class was one of the most delightful classes ever. They, too, were active and excited about peeps. This is the group that will always understand what a flood plain is, as their riverfront homes were damaged and one of their peeps was swept out to sea when the heavy spring rains came. Other peeps have a greater appreciation for insurance, for they had none, and their homes sustained extensive damage and they lost some of the value of their property.

Village is a real-life experience. It treats children as important and offers them a chance to make decisions and to be in control. They see relationships between what they have studied and what they are doing. They are active participants in a learning activity. It is an exciting time for both students and teachers. The teacher gets a chance to see the children in a different way. The class turns to the teacher for information when students need it (certainly a new experience). An interesting rapport develops. Village is a learning experience that leaves both teacher and child feeling excited about education.

The Psychological Significance
of the Game of Village

The progression from creating a peep to creating a primitive shelter and then a permanent home to taking on a professional role within a social community in Village is an accurate summary of many of the tasks of adolescence in

Western cultures. The brilliance of Village is that it has identified the major developmental issues of early adolescence and created forms that allow children to work through these issues in miniature. The reduced scale of the process and the condensed time frame provide a kind of laboratory experience in becoming an adult. Village gives children the opportunity to move from finding a place in the landscape, the task of middle childhood, to shaping and finding a place in the social world, the task of adolescence and adulthood. This process is accomplished in a variety of ways.

Peeps: There is an uncanny similarity between the peeps of the game of Village and the figurine that Jung carved, at around age eleven, and hid in the attic of his house. Jung's figure provided him with a sense of security, an inner calmness in the face of the troubles of the world. In the game of Village, the peep is a similar embodiment of the self. It is representative of the child, but also objectified, separate, and distinct from the child. The peep allows the child to try on different attributes, to try out a "self" without being committed to that character.

During one of the Village sessions, I interviewed a seventeen-year-old junior counselor who had been a "Villager" for many years. When I asked about her peep, she commented:

Rose is a black African writer. She's like me because I like to read a lot of black women writers, but she's different from me because she knows what she's doing, she's older and wiser. Sometimes she surprises me because she'll say things that are important to her but aren't of interest to me. When she talks, I learn things I didn't know about myself.

In commenting about why she liked Village as a twelve-year-old, she recalled:

At that age, I didn't feel like I had any control over things. I knew people expected me to know how things were, but I didn't. Here, I felt like I was in control and everybody was happy because there was a place for everybody and everybody fit in.

Having the focus taken off of you and put onto your peep allows many children to come out of themselves. Similarly, the structure of the game allows each child to find a role and have a place. Children can emerge from their hidden places in the landscape into a social context that is safe—a new matrix.

Building a House: There's an obvious connection between the primitive shelters built for peeps on the homesteading parcel and the forts that children find or build for themselves. As they have shaped spaces for themselves, children immediately warm to making houses for their peeps. Keep in mind here that Jung also places his manikin within a box, a kind of house.

The creation of a real, permanent structure, though miniaturized, is the perfect next step for children at the end of childhood moving into adolescence. You may recall that around age twelve or thirteen, boys in Carriacou changed from making bush houses to making board houses, from primitive shelters to scaled-down models of conventional houses. They were creating places within the community, places to socialize in. Children in Village are invited to go through the same transition. The improved house and grounds become the individual's stake within the structure of the community. This property is eventually evaluated, given literal fiscal value, by all the members of the community. Where on one hand this is an authentic representation of real-world economics, it is also a symbol of the self accruing value or worth in the eyes of peers. Early adolescents desire to be respected and to be valued as unique individuals. This desire is fulfilled through the building of houses, which turn out to be quite different from each other and expressive of the characters of the individuals who conceived them. As the peep represents the personality of the self, the house represents the productiveness of the self.

Taking on a role in the community rounds out this symbolizing of the evolution of the self. Not only is each person's house unique, but each person's talents can be utilized to make the community at large a richer place. Cia Iselin recalls: *"Best of all was one lad, whom no one suspected of having any talents. He achieved instant respect when it was found that he could moderate town meetings."* I am reminded of the children of Buttercombe Close in Devon who created a group den and then the structure of a little society with roles and rules for the members. Village is a success because it provides an articulated vehicle for exploring the world of self in society in a safe but challenging way. This is the kind of transition experience that early adolescents need.

6

THE EVOLUTION OF
A SENSE OF PLACE

A PERSONAL REFLECTION

I have a favorite mile-and-a-half walk in a circuit from my house. Heading east, I walk along the gravel road, past a plantation of red pines and then a sugar bush. Sometimes a barred owl will push ahead of me, down the tunnel of the road. I turn off onto the Monadnock Sunapee trail, rising through hardwoods and then rolling through hemlock and yew. Then the good part: stately old hemlocks line the edge of the trail along Eliza Adams Gorge, a mossy seventy-five-foot-deep cleft with a tannin-stained stream pouring from one pool to the next. In the fall there are many destroying angels here, poisonous white mushrooms luminescent in the late afternoon gloom. There are soft seats in the duff on the edge of the ravine. Before the kids entered our lives, I'd walk the bottom of the ravine, but I haven't done this in three years.

Then out of the darkness into a hilly section of old white pines and mixed hardwoods. Down to Russell Reservoir. Last fall my daughter and I came here on pistachio walks. We sat overlooking the beaver lodge, ate pistachios, and waited for the slap of a tail. Or I'd hide behind big trees and have her find me. The trail then led up past the goat sheds in Dick's field to the road and a short stroll home.

As I left for work during the busy days of February, I kept hearing chainsaw whining from a place where I knew no one would cut cordwood. On the third morning it dawned on me what was happening. I'd written letters a few years ago to discourage a logging project on the piece of land that held the old white pines. When the land was sold to a wealthy older couple, I thought the danger had passed. I hadn't been vigilant enough. Over the next two weeks the saws rang, and the logging trucks pulled away. My wife said they stopped short of the hemlocks, but a third of the trail is now a muddy wash, and slash is everywhere.

I haven't been to see for myself, except from the water when I went canoeing one day. I saw enough to know it won't be a great place for pistachio walks for a number of autumns. Every time I leave the house to go for a walk I consider going down there, but I'm overwhelmed with a sense of sadness and bitterness. That trail had become a special place for me. I had bonded with it, and its wildness, so close to our house, was a kind of treasure. The logging felt like a violation, like when my house was broken into and all my tools were stolen. There was no safe place, no inviolable home. My sense of place had been punctured. I am struck at how I feel personally injured, at how this special place feels like an extension of my body.

BUILDING A COMMITMENT
TO PERSON AND PLACE

The notion of a sense of place has emerged strongly in the past decade among environmentalists. In *A Sense of Place: The Artist and the American Land*, Alan Gussow defines place as *"a piece of the environment that has been claimed by feelings. We are homesick for places. . . . And the catalyst that converts any physical location into a place is the process of experiencing deeply."*[1] To experience a place deeply is to bond with a place.

The roots of the adult notion of a sense of place are established during middle childhood. Rachel Carson's *sense of wonder* of early childhood gets transmuted in middle childhood to a *sense of exploration*.[2] Children leave the security of home behind and set out, like Alice in Wonderland and Columbus and Robinson Crusoe, to discover the new world. In the process, children create new homes, homes away from home. These homes become the new safe place, a small world that they create from the raw materials of the natural world and their flexible imaginations. This new home in the wilds and the journeys of discovering are the basis for bonding with the natural world. As we bonded with our parents in the early years, we bond with Mother Earth in middle childhood.

The significant world, the world that we are bonded to, expands outward as we grow older. The infant's world is the enclosed space between its mother's arms. The world then becomes the house, the neighborhood, the community, the bioregion, the nation, and perhaps, eventually, the globe. Through the successive stages of human development we maintain our old relationships but move outward to bond to new spheres of significance. If this process is to continue ever expanding, then each bonding must occur in sequence. Feeling a sense of place in adulthood leads us to a commitment to preserve the integrity of the communities we live in. Developing this sense of place depends on the previous bonding of the child to the nearby natural world in middle childhood. The sense of place is born in child-ren's special places.

Education in harmony with development should, among other things, create adults with both a sense of individual initiative and a sense of responsibility to the natural and social worlds. How do we accomplish this? One small way we can help is to acknowledge, in our education, the world-making tendencies of the individual. In middle childhood this means allowing the child to find and create private worlds. If we allow children to shape their own small worlds in childhood, then they will grow up knowing and feeling that they can participate in shap-ing the big world tomorrow.

NOTES

Chapter 1

1. Roger Hart, *Children's Experience of Place* (New York: Irvington, 1979).

Chapter 2

1. Roger Hart, *Children's Experience of Place* (New York: Irvington, 1979).

2. Ibid.

Chapter 3

1. Joseph Chilton Pearce, *Magical Child* (New York: E. P. Dutton, 1977).

2. Annie Dillard, *An American Childhood* (New York: Harper and Row, 1987).

3. Carl Jung, *Memories, Dreams, Reflections* (New York: Pantheon Books, 1961).

4. Edith Newlin Chase, "Secret Dawn," in *Small Window Panes* (Goshen, N.H.: Phineas Press, 1978).

5. Clare Cooper Marcus, "The House as a Symbol of the Self." In *Designing for Human Behavior,* ed. Jon Lang et al. (Stroudsberg, Pa.: Dowden, Hutchinson and Ross, 1974).

6. Jung, *Memories, Dreams, Reflections.*

7. Marcus, "The House as a Symbol of the Self."

Chapter 4

1. Edith Cobb, "The Ecology of Imagination in Childhood," *The Subversive Science: Essays towards an Ecology of Man.* Edited by Paul Shepard and Daniel McKinley (Boston: Houghton Mifflin, 1969).

2. Ibid.

3. Ibid.

4. Rosanne McCarthy, "Childhood Memory." Unpublished paper in the author's collection, 1988.

5. Catherine Sprague, "Small Worlds." Unpublished paper in the author's collection, 1989.

6. Cobb, "The Ecology of Imagination in Childhood."

7. Louise Chawla, "Ecstatic Places." *Children's Environments Quarterly* 7, 4 (1990): 18–23, and "The Ecology of Environmental Memory." *Children's Environments Quarterly* 3, 4 (1986): 34–42.

8. Ibid.

9. See Edward Robinson, *The Original Vision: A Study of the Religious Experience of Childhood* (New York: The Seabury Press, 1983).

10. Robinson, *The Original Vision*.

11. Lisa Murrow, "Living in the City: A Rural Family's Point of View," *City Childhood Newsletter* 18 (1970).

12. Bonnie Baron, "Escape behind the Billboards." Unpublished paper in the author's collection, 1990.

13. Nancy Segreto, response to the questionnaire "Dens, Forts, Hideouts, and Playhouses," in the author's collection.

14. Catherine Sprague, response to the questionnaire "Dens, Forts, Hideouts, and Playhouses," in the author's collection.

15. Roger Hart, *Children's Experience of Place* (New York: Irvington, 1979).

16. Robert Arbib, *The Lord's Woods* (New York: W. W. Norton and Co., 1971).

17. Carole Riley, "Laurie's 'Saga of Jamestown.'" In *Children's Landscapes*. Unpublished paper in the author's collection, 1977.

18. Tina Staller, interview with the author.

19. Marcia King, "Reflections on Betwixt and Between." Unpublished paper in the author's collection, 1989.

20. Carole Riley, *Children's Landscapes*.

21. Mary Morrisette, interview with the author.

22. Catherine Sprague, response to the questionnaire "Dens, Forts, Hideouts, and Playhouses."

23. Nancy Segreto, response to the questionnaire "Dens, Forts, Hideouts, and Playhouses."

24. See Kim Stafford, "The Separate Hearth." In *Having Everything Right: Essays of Place* (Lewiston, Idaho: Confluence Press, 1986). Subsequent quotes are from Stafford's book.

Chapter 5

1. Janet Altobell, "A Home in the Woods," *Harris Hearsay* vol. 14, no. 1 (1991).

2. Kimberly Dovey, "The Life and Death of Arlington Huts," *Children's Environments Quarterly* vol. 4, no. 4 (1987).

3. Patrice O'Neill Maynard, "The Forts at the George C. Soule School" (Unpublished paper).

4. Ibid.

5. Ibid.

6. Cornelia Iselin, *The Game of Village Handbook* (Nelson, N.H.: Spectrum Productions, 1987).

7. Ibid.

Chapter 6

1. Alan Gussow, *A Sense of Place: The Artist and the American Land* (San Francisco: Friends of the Earth, 1972).

2. Rachel Carson, *A Sense of Wonder* (New York: Harper Collins, 1999).

BIBLIOGRAPHY

Altobell, Janet. "A Home in the Woods." *Harris Hearsay,* vol. 14, no. 1. Hancock, N.H.: 1991.

Arbib, Robert. *The Lord's Woods.* New York: W. W. Norton and Co., 1971.

Bachelard, Gaston. *The Poetics of Space.* Boston: Beacon Press, 1969.

Baron, Bonnie. "Escape behind the Billboards." Unpublished paper in the author's collection, 1990.

Carson, Rachel. *A Sense of Wonder.* New York, HarperCollins, 1999.

Chase, Edith Newlin. "Secret Dawn." In *Small Window Panes.* Goshen, N.H.: Phineas Press, 1978.

Chawla, Louise. "The Ecology of Environmental Memory." *Children's Environments Quarterly* 3, 4 (1986): 34–42.

—. "Ecstatic Places." *Children's Environments Quarterly* 7, 4 (1990): 18–23.

Cobb, Edith. "The Ecology of Imagination in Childhood." *The Subversive Science: Essays towards an Ecology of Man*, edited by Paul Shepard and Daniel McKinley (Boston: Houghton Mifflin, 1969).

Dovey, Kimberly. "The Life and Death of Arlington Huts." *Children's Environments Quarterly*, vol. 4, no. 4. New York: Center for Human Environments, 1987.

George, Jean Craighead. *My Side of the Mountain*. New York: E. P. Dutton, 1959.

Gussow, Alan. *A Sense of Place: The Artist and American Land*. San Francisco: Friends of the Earth, 1972.

Hart, Roger A. *Children's Experience of Place*. New York: Irvington Publishers, Inc., 1979.

Iselin, Cornelia. *The Game of Village Handbook*. Nelson, N.H.: Spectrum Productions, 1987.

Jung, Carl. *Memories, Dreams, Reflections*. New York: Pantheon Books, 1961.

King, Marcia. "Reflection on Betwixt and Between." Unpublished paper in the author's collection, 1989.

McCarthy, Roseanne. "Childhood Memory." Unpublished paper in the author's collection, 1988.

McLerran, Alice. *Roxaboxen*. New York: Lothrop, Lee, and Shepard, 1991.

Marcus, Clare Cooper. "The House as a Symbol of the Self." In *Designing for Human Behavior.* Edited by Jon Lang, et al. Stroudsberg, Pa.: Dowden, Hutchinson, and Ross, 1974.

Maynard, Patrice O'Neill. "The Forts at the George C. Soule School." Unpublished paper in the author's collection, 1990.

Middlebrooks, Sally. *Getting to Know City Kids: Understanding Their Thinking, Imagining, and Socializing.* New York: Teacher's College Press, 1998.

Murphy, Dick. Unpublished writings of fifth-grade children.

Murrow, Lisa. "Living in the City: A Rural Family's Point of View." *City Childhood Newsletter no. 18.* New York: Center for Human Environments, 1979.

Pearce, Joseph Chilton. *Magical Child.* New York: E. P. Dutton, 1977.

Riley, Carole. *Children's Landscapes.* Unpublished paper in the author's collection, 1977.

Robinson, Edward. *The Original Vision: A Study of the Religious Experience of Childhood.* New York: The Seabury Press, 1983.

Segreto, Nancy. Response to the questionnaire "Dens, Forts, Hideouts, and Playhouses." In the author's collection.

Sprague, Catherine. "Small Worlds." Unpublished paper in the author's collection, 1989.

—. Response to the questionnaire "Dens, Forts, Hideouts, and Playhouses." In the author's collection.

Stafford, Kim. "The Separate Hearth." *Having Everything Right: Essays of Place.* Lewiston, Idaho: Confluence Press, 1986.

Stevens, Sally. "The Children's Village." Unpublished paper in the author's collection, 1990.

Sullwold, Edith. "The Ritual Maker Within," in *Betwixt and Between: Patterns of Masculine and Feminine Initiation.* La Salle, Ill.: Open Court, 1987.